GETTING IN

ACCOUNTANCY
BUSINESS STUDIES &
ECONOMICS

TROTMAN

This edition published in 1994
by Trotman and Company Ltd,
12 Hill Rise, Richmond, Surrey TW10 6UA

© Trotman and Company Limited 1994

British Library Cataloguing in Publication Data
A catalogue record for this book is available from
the British Library.

ISBN 0 85660 241 8

Printed in Great Britain by Redwood Books,
Trowbridge, Wiltshire

CONTENTS

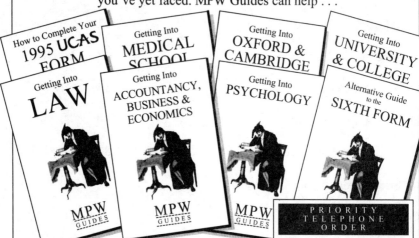

PREFACE

The past few years has seen an increase in the number of sixth-formers applying to universities for degree courses in Accountancy, Business Studies and Economics. At MPW we have gathered together a mass of information about these courses and now, with the help and encouragement of Trotman & Co., it has been possible to supplement this information with external research and bring it all together in this guide.

I am very grateful to Sue O'Connell who did the external research and to Stephen Skillman who put that research in to the published format. Thanks are also due to Alastair Boag, a personal tutor at MPW in London, who wrote the general advice on filling in your UCAS form and preparing for interviews and to Chris Heaton of BPP Courses Ltd who wrote the section explaining the work of accountants.

I hope that, as you research courses in Accountancy, Business Studies and Economics, you will find what we have written helpful and that you will let us have your comments and suggestions for the next edition.

Joe Ruston
September 1994

ABOUT THIS BOOK

☐ INTRODUCTION

Careers in finance are generally better rewarded in purely financial terms than those in other sectors of the economy. If you're hoping to get into Accountancy, Business or Economics this guide is here to help you.

You'll see that the book is divided into four main sections:

- First there's a brief guide to working in accountancy, business and economics: what it involves and how to get there.

- The second section – and the bulk of the book – is devoted to a consideration of Higher Education courses in Accountancy, Business Studies and Economics in the UK. The factors you should be thinking about when working out which courses you should apply for are discussed. We've also got a comprehensive listing of all courses in Accountancy, Business Studies and Economics in the UK at the back of the book. Symbols show you what type of campus the course is based at. Statistics show you how likely you are to get on to the course you apply for and indicate how employable you're likely to be having studied at a particular institution. You can also see, at a glance, what grades you'll need to get to win a place on a specific course.

- The third section tells you how to fill in your UCAS form and advises you on how you can prepare for an interview.

- The fourth section contains a brief summary of some of the current issues in the worlds of accountancy, business and economics. You can use this as a starter in preparing for an interview or simply to get an idea of what's going on.

If that isn't enough you'll find several lists at the end of the book – lists of addresses of all the universities and colleges in the tables so you'll know where to write off for prospectuses, and lists of professional institutions you can write to for further details of the career paths mentioned in the text. You'll also find comments from a number of leading employers and a reading list if you want to find out more about anything raised in the book.

We've included a series of exercises and a questionnaire you can use to find out which courses you'll need more information on and which courses you should be putting on to your UCAS form. We've included everything we can think of that will help you get into Accountancy, Business Studies or Economics.

Finally, if there's anything else we could have put in – that you'd have found useful – or if there's anything that's confused you, please let us know.

Chapter 1
WHAT DO ACCOUNTANTS DO?

☐ THE PROFESSION OF ACCOUNTANCY

The gaining of a professional qualification in accountancy opens the door to a progressive career in any one of several fields. These include working in accountancy practice, in industry, in commerce, or in the public sector. There is a high percentage of managing directors and chief executives, in both public and private sectors, with an accountancy background. The career prospects for a professionally qualified accountant are excellent.

There are many misconceptions about accountants: images of introverted bean counters compiling ledgers with quill pens still abound. They are totally unjustified! The accountancy world of today is challenging, dynamic and offers excellent opportunities to suit the aspirations of most students.

In general terms, an accountant increasingly requires business and communication skills as well as the ability to generate and analyse data. The particular type of work you'll undertake both in training and after qualification depends on which of the four sorts of accountancy you choose. Each of the four is represented by a professional body.

Chartered Accountancy

Chartered Accountants offer a wide range of services. The type of work you do and the environment you work in depends very much on the size of firm you work for. If you join one of the large international firms, the so called 'Big 6', you will spend most of your time in either Audit or Tax. Auditing is checking whether the accounts produced by a company show a true and fair picture of its financial performance and status. Most of this work is done at clients' offices and requires not only technical expertise but also business acumen and inter-personal skills. With large clients you could well be involved in several locations both nationally and internationally.

Working in the tax department involves dealing with clients, calculating their tax liabilities, providing them with tax planning, and negotiating on their behalf with the Inland Revenue.

If you join one of the smaller or medium sized firms you'll enjoy a greater range both of work and of clients. For smaller clients you'll be doing accountancy work (helping them prepare their books), as well as audit, tax, and often business planning. You'll also come into contact sooner than you would in a large firm with the senior people both within your firm and at the clients. However, you won't be dealing with large public companies or the complexities and sophistication offered by that environment.

As well as accountancy, audit and tax you may be able to move into insolvency work during your training period. This challenging environment requires practical business skills and good legal knowledge as you strive to rescue ailing businesses or to sort through the debris of collapsed companies.

Working for a firm of Chartered Accountants is therefore very varied and much depends on your choice of firm. It is also now possible to undertake your training within other organisations such as Unilever and the National Audit Office which are registered for training. You will not be visiting clients, but placements will see you operating in different internal departments such as audit, tax, treasury and finance.

Starting salaries for trainee Chartered Accountants vary with the training office's location and size. In London salaries start around £12,500- £17,000 whilst those in provincial offices run from £10,000.

Certified Accountancy

Certified Accountants may operate in all fields of employment: industry, commerce, practice and in the public sector. The work experience gained during training depends largely on the employer. Certified Accountants in practice will undertake much the same role as Chartered Accountants in smaller practices. (See above for details.)

In industry and commerce you'll be involved in the preparation of financial accounts and in the provision of management accounting information. This includes work on costing and budgeting – the management accounts are used by management to make key business decisions.

In the public sector (local and central government, health authorities, transport executives etc.) you'll be doing much the same sort of work – providing management accounting information, costing and budgeting – but with substantially bigger budgets.

Starting salaries for those joining industrial and commercial companies range from £12,000 to £15,000. For those joining practice or public sector organisations the starting salaries are a little lower.

Management Accountants

In common with Certified Accountants, you'll be working to provide financially based management information which is essential to the planning and running of a business. This will almost certainly be in industry or commerce. You will also be involved, from an early stage, with project work which may involve spending periods of time within different, non-accountancy departments. It is quite likely that you will assume a managerial role before you qualify.

Management Accountancy, therefore, appeals to those who are interested in business, in the running of a business and in general management as well as in finance and financial management.

Starting salaries range from £10,000 to £16,000 depending on location and size of company.

Public sector accountancy

Working and training in the public sector is the most specialised form of accountancy. Notionally you will be undertaking similar tasks as other accountants such as preparing accounts and budgets, processing accounting information, monitoring and analysing expenditure and investment, and also audit.

However, the environment is very different. The sums involved will be large (up to £1 billion) and the underlying purposes of the organisations are different: they will be providing a service to the public, profit will not be a consideration. However, value for money and cost effectiveness are vital in today's environment: this will provide a stimulating challenge. You'll also be able to work in different areas: depending on your choice there could be health, education, leisure, social services, housing, planning etc.

Starting salaries range from £10,000 to £13,000 depending upon the employer.

☐ HOW TO BECOME AN ACCOUNTANT

There are a number of ways of qualifying as an accountant. A generalised view of the path to qualification is shown below. If you're interested in more specific details – entry requirements etc. – you should contact the professional bodies (you'll find their addresses at the end of the book).

A generalised view of the paths to becoming an accountant.

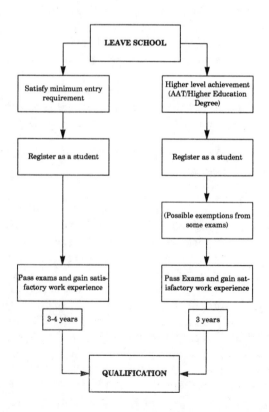

If your sights are set on becoming an accountant as soon as possible you have two options:

1. You can start training immediately you finish school – if you've got the right qualifications. You'd take 3-4 years to complete training and examinations and be professionally qualified aged 21-22.

2. You can go into Higher Education and try to get the maximum exemptions from your professional exams during your course – you'll need to check the course details very carefully. It'd also be a good idea to confirm with the relevant professional body that you will, in fact, be exempt from the papers in question. Although this route would take 5-6 years from leaving school you'd have a degree at the end of it, as well as the professional qualification.

The classic route into accountancy for graduates is to join a firm of Chartered Accountants as a graduate trainee. Unbelievably this path is followed by about 10% of all graduates. If you're thinking of becoming a graduate trainee then try and find out if there are any options you can take while on your course – even if it's nothing to do with accountancy – that could exempt you from some of the professional exam papers.

Whichever path you decide to take you will be signing up for around three years' further hard work before gaining the professional qualification. Once qualified you must undertake CPE (Continuing Professional Education) to satisfy the membership requirements of your governing body.

When you have passed your final qualifying exams and satisfied other relevant requirements you will be entitled to add some more initials to your surname and to call yourself a Chartered Accountant or a Certified Accountant etc.

It's been said before but if you're serious about becoming an accountant then the best thing you can do is to contact the professional bodies (their addresses are given at the end of this book), find which type of accountancy is right for you and then work out what's the best way for you to become that sort of accountant.

☐ OTHER OPTIONS

Gaining a professional qualification takes time and can cost a lot of money. Equally many people study accountancy with no intention of ever becoming a professional accountant. One of the great advantages of an accountancy degree, however, is that it provides the student with the fundamentals of the language of accountancy. Many accountancy students will not enter the profession but will use their degree to pursue work in other areas. The table below shows you the first destination of 1990 Accountancy graduates. If you choose to study accountancy you can always consider other options.

TABLE SHOWING FIRST DESTINATIONS OF ACCOUNTANCY GRADUATES (1990)

Total graduating

Unemployed	104
Teacher training	6
Other training	57
Research etc.	19
Short-term UKemployment	51
Permanent UKemployment	1245
Total graduating	1,943

Type of work

Administration and operational management	38
Marketing etc.	16
Management services, computing	11
Financial work	1,150
Personnel/social etc.	6

Employers

Accountancy	864
Banking/insurance	66
Industry	112
'Other' commerce	58
Local government	52
Civil Service	10

It is also very true that a substantial proportion of students who have not studied accountancy go on, after graduation, into accountancy training contracts. If you're not sure that you want to be an accountant it's not the end of the world if you choose to study something else at University – as long as you do well at it.

Chapter 2
WHAT IS BUSINESS AND HOW DO I GET INTO IT?

☐ WHAT IS BUSINESS AND HOW DO I GET INTO IT?

A business is, essentially, a machine which exists to fulfil a purpose decided by its owner. Most companies exist to produce wealth for their owners. At one end of the business scale are public companies, often multinationals, which produce dividends and capital growth for their shareholders. At the other end of the scale, small businesses may exist as a source of income for their owners; sometimes profit is a subsidiary motive to an owner's enthusiasm for working in a particular way or in a particular field – you must have visited second-hand bookshops!

The components of the machine are its employees. As a graduate you'll have gained a variety of skills which are of value in the world of business – the ability to communicate effectively; to research, analyse and present information; to work to deadlines and to work under pressure. These skills can be used in a variety of business functions – Marketing, Sales, Personnel, Finance and General Management. In most of these areas you'll be able to gain professional qualifications on which to found your career.

☐ SO WHAT DO THEY ALL DO?

Marketing

Marketing tends to attract people who have some sort of creative talent. The marketing expert must try to make people aware that a product exists.

A recent TV ad for Pepsi features two chimps in a laboratory being tested for improvements in response skills after drinking two different brands of cola. The non-Pepsi chimp was seen surrounded by scientists putting, with some difficulty, square pegs into holes. The Pepsi chimp, on the other hand, was discovered enjoying the sun in the back of a jeep with plenty of girlfriends and was, of course, drinking Pepsi.

Such ads require considerable planning and market research. The marketing people will have researched the product and its rivals and identified how and where they want to 'place' their product in the market in order to maximise sales, or brand loyalty, market penetration etc. They'll have commissioned an advertising agency to come up with a suitable advertisement and monitored how advertising affected sales.

Psychologists are often involved in devising advertising slogans or images that will stick in the mind and which will be recalled or will influence us when we see the product. For Pepsi the advertisers wanted customers to associate Pepsi with 'fun'.

Careers in marketing are often varied: many people who have worked in marketing later move on to advertising agencies or to work as publicity consultants.

Sales

Another aspect of business is sales. This work is increasingly commission only i.e. if you don't sell anything you don't get paid. On the other hand, if you're good at selling the rewards can be fantastic. You can be taught sales techniques as part of a business studies course but selling seems to come more 'naturally' to some than others.

What you sell will depend on the business. Books, advertising, professional services, time-shares, stocks and shares, ideas, cars – anything that a business produces needs to be sold. If you're not sure, then your summer vacations could be a useful testing period.

Personnel

As a personnel officer you'd be involved in the recruitment and training of staff, in implementing both company policies and government legislation affecting employees and in maintaining employee records.

Personnel work is often challenging and can be very rewarding.

Finance

The financial aspects of a business are commonly regarded as the most important. If there's no cash in the tills and the bank wants the overdraft repaid yesterday – that's trouble.

In finance you'd be involved in all aspects of budgeting, monitoring cashflows, evaluating projects etc. There's more information of these aspects in Chapter 1.

Purchasing

If one side of profit is making sales then equally important is that what's sold has been bought cheaply.

In an increasingly free market, the role of purchasing professionals is growing more important. The larger the organisation the more likely it is to be involved in 'big buck' negotiations. Purchasing professionals investigate sources of raw materials, compare different sources, negotiate for discounts, check for quality, maintain good relationships with suppliers – generally supervising all aspects of expenditure on raw materials and consumables.

General Management

Several large businesses have openings for both school-leavers and graduates as management trainees.

You'd usually expect a formalised training programme – if you do see one, this should provide some evidence of the professionalism of the organisation. Most schemes give an initial period of training where you receive placements in a number of departments within the organisation – finance, sales and marketing for example. At the end of this period you decide where you want to specialise. A number of companies have fast-stream management programmes with accelerated training and early responsibility.

the
MANCHESTER
METROPOLITAN
UNIVERSITY

Meeting your future needs

with over 300 courses in 50 different subject areas...
...one of them will be right for you.

Our mission is to be an accessible institution of higher education meeting the educational and vocational needs of our students and our partners in industry, commerce and the professions.

Being Britain's largest University, we are able to offer an unparalleled choice of undergraduate, postgraduate and professional courses, most of which reflect a primary but not exclusive orientation towards some form of practical education with strong vocational links. We also have an extensive portfolio of research and consultancy activities.

Many of our courses are available in both full-time and part-time modes and a Credit Accumulation & Transfer Scheme (CATS) offers further flexibility and choice.

We have an excellent library, computing and accommodation facilities and our Students' Union offers an extensive range of sporting and recreational activities. We provide a student welfare service which can assist with accommodation, study skills development, personal and financial problems and also provides a careers advice service.

Our main location is in the centre of Manchester, a city renowned for its thriving cultural, social and sporting life. Manchester has been designated Britain's "City of Drama" for 1994 and has some of the most up to date sporting facilities in the country, including a purpose built velodrome. Some of Britain's most beautiful countryside and many other attractions and facilities lie within easy reach of the city.

The former Crewe + Alsager College of Higher Education, located in the Cheshire countryside became a faculty of the University in 1992.

For more information call our 24 hour prospectus hot-line: 061-247 1055, or write to us: The Manchester Metropolitan University, All Saints, Manchester M15 6BH.

Be a little mercenary at university.

This isn't a call for soldiers of fortune. (Money, let's face it, should never be the prime motivation for joining the Forces.)

It's the chance for school leavers, torn between university and the Army, to get the best of both worlds.

All you have to do is meet the challenge of our three-day Officer Selection Board.

Then we'll pay you a total of £25,000 to complete your course at either university or college of higher education, providing you agree to serve as an Officer for at least five years after you graduate.

That means you'll have three times as much to spend as the average student. With the promise of a demanding and exciting job once you've got your Degree.

If you only wish to commit yourself for three years, you can simply apply for a special £1,200 p.a. bursary to supplement any existing grants. But what if you're already halfway through your course?

Providing you have at least one year left to study, you can still benefit from either scheme.

For the full details, just complete the coupon below. And find out how to remain permanently at peace with your bank manager.

For more information about Army Cadetships, please telephone 0345 300111 at any time and quote 0432 (charged at local call rate). Or post this coupon to: Major John Gutteridge, Army Officer Sponsorship, Freepost 4335, Dept. 0432, Bristol BS1 3YX.

Full name_____

_____ BLOCK CAPITALS PLEASE

Address_____

_____

_____ Postcode_____

Date of birth_____ Nationality_____

Army Officer

☐ SMALL BUSINESSES

There's no reason why you shouldn't work for a small business. You are unlikely to have very specific responsibilities; you won't be assigned to any departments – there probably won't be separate departments to be assigned to. You should, however, get first-hand experience of the prizes and pitfalls of a career in business. You'll be immediately aware of the differences that effective marketing makes and will gain first-hand experience of things like dealing with banks and coping with disgruntled customers – the day-to-day business of business.

☐ SETTING UP YOUR OWN

There's no reason why you shouldn't set up your own business either. If you've got a good idea, have some experience of constructing cashflow forecasts and don't fear failure or hard work then this could be your route into the world of business. Richard Branson started his empire while still as school – as did Alan Sugar. Anita Roddick and Terence Conran both started international companies from small businesses. Do remember though that if entrepreneurs succeed at all it is usually having learnt from two or three previous failures. There doesn't seem to be such a thing as 'Beginners' Luck'.

☐ HOW A BUSINESS STUDIES COURSE FITS IN

By taking a course in Business Studies you could get a head start into the world of business over other graduates. Some courses are biased towards particular areas such as marketing or personnel. If you already have an interest in a particular area of business then look for courses where this interest will be drawn out.

However, it does have to be said that about 40% of vacancies advertised for graduates don't ask for a specific degree subject. Many potential employers are more interested in the class of degree than in its subject. If you do want to get into business but don't want to take Business Studies it shouldn't matter that much – as long as you do well in what you do.

☐ GETTING INTO THE WORLD OF BUSINESS

You are an individual with your own set of abilities and the various skills you've picked up along the way. The most important thing is that you know them and can demonstrate how you've put them to use. Employers in business look for aptitude, promise, evidence of an interest in business or, better, in a specific area of business. If you're thinking of setting up on your own you'll need to be innovative and creative, energetic and resilient, persistent and prepared to work long hours, realistic in your business plans and able to adapt rapidly to changing circumstances – in addition to having all the relevant business skills.

☐ IF I TAKE BUSINESS STUDIES WHAT SORT OF WORK WOULD I DO?

The table opposite shows the destination of 1992 Business/Management Studies graduates. It shows the diversity of paths after graduation.

Of those graduates in full-time employment the most popular areas of employment are in Financial Work and in Sales and Marketing. It seems that, if you want to get into these areas of employment, Business Studies is a good thing to do.

TABLE SHOWING FIRST DESTINATIONS OF BUSINESS/MANAGEMENT STUDIES GRADUATES (1992)

Total graduating	Percentage
Not available	4.50
Unemployed	12.70
Overseas students leaving U.K.	13.10
Overseas employment	2.80
Teacher training	1.00
Other training	3.30
Further academic study	4.60
Short-term UK employment	8.40
Permanent UK employment	49.70
Total	**100.00**

Type of work	
Administration and operational management	20.60
Environmental planning, construction	3.00
Sales, marketing, buying	24.90
Management services, computing	4.90
Financial work	27.40
Others (includes all categories with under 3%)	19.20
Total	**100.00**

Chapter 3
A CAREER IN ECONOMICS

'Economists advise government, financial institutions, industrial companies and international organisations on the economic aspects of policy, investment, demand, resource planning and related topics. The competition for some of these posts is very keen and a higher degree could be appropriate.' – *AGCAS careers booklet, Management Services, Economic and Statistical Work*

This is not to discourage you if your heart is set on being an economist. Be encouraged – to work hard and to get there.

When you do get there, what'll you be doing?

The Government Economic Service employs about 450 economists. Their jobs range from macro-economic analyses of current trends in, for example, the balance of payments to micro-economic analyses of, for example, performance measurement in the education system.

In industry and commerce, economists work on things such as the advantages of changing the source of supply of raw materials; they'll consider the broader implications of a company's policy. In financial institutions too, economists assess things strategically – evaluating how events outside an organisation will affect the organisation. As an economist you might be evaluating the effects of recession on your company's Balance Sheet and cashflows.

There are several areas of employment, other than as a pure economist, for which an economics degree is both relevant and useful. The skills of the economics graduate in the selection and analysis of data and in the use of words and figures to argue a case are well recognised. In addition to these skills, the knowledge acquired during the degree course often leads to exemptions from certain professional exams – such as those in Accountancy.

☐ WHAT DO ECONOMICS GRADUATES DO?

The table shows the destination of 1992 economics graduates. It shows that few Economics graduates find employment as economists but that most end up in financial work.

As mentioned at the start of this chapter, there's always the alternative of studying for a higher degree which, in Economics, could lead to some plum jobs.

TABLE SHOWING THE FIRST DESTINATION OF ECONOMICS GRADUATES (1992)

Total graduating	Percentage
Not available	5.4
Unemployed	13.8
Overseas students leaving U.K.	12.9
Overseas employment	1.9
Teacher training	2.4
Other training	5.0
Further academic study	14.3
Short-term UK employment	7.6
Permanent UK employment	36.6
Total	**100**

Type of work	
Administration and operational management	11.2
Sales, marketing, buying	10.5
Management services, computing	4.3
Financial work	49.7
Information, library, museum work	4.0
Others (includes all categories with under 3%	20.3
Total	**100.00%**

Chapter 4
CHOOSING YOUR COURSE

If you've read the first three chapters you should have some idea of what it's like to work as an accountant, business man or woman, or as an economist. When you have read this chapter you will be in a good position to fill in your UCAS form – the first step towards getting into your chosen field.

There are a huge number of courses available in each of the three subjects. To help you choose which one is right for you we guide you through the planning process and consider the factors you should think about when choosing which one is right for you.

In the Tables section, p 63, you'll find a questionnaire designed to help narrow down your choice. There is also a decision grid which you can use to prioritise your courses and to work out which eight you should put on your UCAS form and in which order you should put them. A sample letter has also been written for you – of the type you should send when requesting a prospectus. Any reference to **the tables** means the tables at the back of the book.

☐ PLANNING

The stereotypical image of sixth form life may be one of chaos – an unrevised exam to sit tomorrow and three projects to be typed and submitted yesterday! But it's really in your best interests to be organised and get your selections sorted out early. The notes below should give you a rough idea of what you should be doing at various stages.

During the last term of your lower sixth year

May/June :
Do some serious thinking. Get ideas from friends, relatives, teachers, books etc. If possible visit some universities. Attend the Higher Education fairs.

June-August:
Lay your hands on copies of the official and alternative (ie student written) prospectuses and departmental brochures for extra details. They are usually in libraries but it's more reliable to get your own sent to you. Make a shortlist of your courses with the help of this guide.

During your upper sixth year

September:
Fill out your application form and give it to your referee for sending off to UCAS – it will be accepted from 1 September onwards.

15 December:
This is the deadline for submitting your applications to UCAS. If you wanted to apply to Oxford or Cambridge then you should have put your form in before 15 October. UCAS will still consider late applications, but your chances are limited since some of the places have already gone.

November:
The nail-biting starts. Universities hold their interviews and/or open days and start to send out their decisions directly to the candidates.

15 May *at the latest:*
Or within two weeks of the final decision you receive, you must tell UCAS (assuming you've had some offers) which offer you have accepted firmly and which one is your back-up.

Summer:	Sit your exams and await the results! After you get them wait a bit longer and by the end of August you'll know if you've been accepted by a university or college. Don't be too disappointed if you haven't got in. Just get in touch with your school, college or careers office and hang on until September when the left-over places will be filled through 'clearing'. It's up to you to get hold of the published list of these places and contact the universities directly by yourself.

For full details of the UCAS procedure see *How to complete your 1995 UCAS form* (details in the reading list on page 56).

☐ CHOOSING YOUR COURSE

This chapter will help you make your choice of 15 courses by encouraging you to focus on certain key factors. These are:

- Where do you want to study?
- What sort of environment do you want to study in?
- How employable will you be at the end of the course?
- What kind of course are you after?
- Qualification gained
- Course length
- Will your A-levels be good enough?
- Statistics
- Quality of teaching

We'll go through each of these factors in turn. You'll be asked to consider those that you think are important. Then we'll go through the tables and choose the courses that you'll put on your UCAS form.

To help you choose the courses to put on your UCAS form there's a questionnaire which you can fill in.

Tip: You will find it helpful to scan through the questionnaire and worked example on pp. 63-68 before you read on.

⬜ WHERE DO YOU WANT TO STUDY?

Some students don't put much stress on this and are fairly geographically mobile, preferring instead to choose the degree course and see where they end up. But university life isn't going to be solely about academic study. Anyone who tells you that hasn't been to university themselves! It is truly a growing experience – educationally, socially, culturally – and besides, three years can really drag if you're not happy outside the lecture theatre.

The first two columns in the tables at the back of the book tell you which area and at which institution the course is in. If you're not sure where the areas are here's a map to show you.

1	LONDON
2	SOUTH-EAST ENGLAND
3	SOUTH-WEST ENGLAND
4	THE MIDLANDS
5	EAST ENGLAND
6	NORTH-EAST ENGLAND
7	NORTH-WEST ENGLAND
8	NORTHERN IRELAND
9	SCOTLAND
10	WALES

What follows is an assortment of factors which might have some bearing on where you'd like to study – see which ones you think are relevant to you.

- Friends and family: do you want to get away or stay close to them? Whilst you may like the challenge of looking after yourself and the opportunity to be completely independent, there are definitely advantages to living near home, assuming that home is fairly accessible for you – not least of which are travel costs between home and university.

- The cost of living in the area. Will you be able to reach deeper into your pockets for rent or other fundamentals and entertainment if you are living in a major city or in 'the South'?

- What sort of accommodation are you likely to live in there? Is it important to you to live on campus or in halls of residence with other students, or in private housing that you may need to organise yourself and may be a considerable distance from college? Are you a self-catering kind of person? Perhaps you would prefer it if someone else cooked for you. Is there any point in moving away from home?

- Urban or rural, large or small? Do you yearn for concrete and noise pollution, or would you kill for trees and birdsong? In practice of course, many universities combine the convenience of the city with the atmosphere of the countryside by locating their campus just on the edge of a major town eg University of Nottingham, University of Canterbury etc. But size is a different story. Larger universities may well have better facilities and bigger budgets, but they can overwhelm some students who would be better off in a smaller place where they can at least feel some sense of community.

- What are facilities like in and around the university? Apart from the academic resources, which should be all important to prospective students, are you going to be spending much time in, for example, the sports' centre? Are you a theatre-goer or clubber? How about the societies within the student body? Is there one for you to indulge your own hobbies be they common-or-garden or positively bizarre? And if there isn't anything, then would you really be that disappointed?

• Life after graduation. Yes, there is some, and if you are set on working in a certain area then you may want to study close to that place. If nothing else, you won't have far to move after graduation.

Some of the comments you might have heard regarding location of university are:

'London is expensive, and the colleges are all spread out in different areas.'
'I set my heart on going to Oxford.'
'At the time there were only two places offering the Business & French course I wanted to take.'

Some students are very clear about where they want to study. Look at the list above, and then tick the 'No' box on question 1 of the questionnaire for any areas you definitely don't want to study in and cross them off the diagram below.

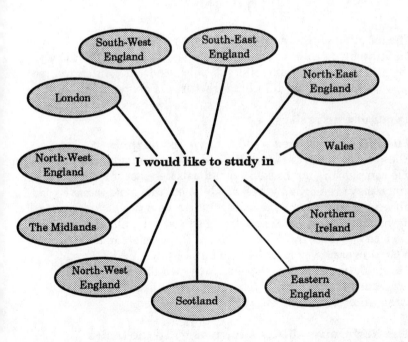

Cross out any areas where you wouldn't like to study

If you already know where you plan to study you can eliminate nine of the ten regions straightaway.

A word of warning here: it is tempting to assert your independence by moving as far away from your home as possible. If you do, you'll have to take into consideration things like the cost, the isolation and maybe the difficulty of getting home when you want to – many students don't move more than 100 miles from their home. If you'd like to stay near your home, pick the area you're living in at the moment – if you're close to the border of other areas, pick them too. For example, if you're interested in South East England, consider London and the Midlands as well.

Now enter your decision in section 1 of the questionnaire on page 63.

☐ WHAT SORT OF ENVIRONMENT DO YOU WANT TO STUDY IN?

The question of where to study also encompasses the sort of institution you want to attend. There are many ways of classifying the different sorts of university. We'll consider the different types of universitites and the different structures of universities.

Types of University

The Old Universities – shown as • in the tables
These cover both rural and city sites, but traditionally are set on just one campus and not broken up and splattered over a wide area. Since they are normally well established, they tend to have good libraries and research facilities. Old Universities have a reputation for being resilient to change, but they are gradually introducing modern elements into their degrees. This is more in line with the New Universities, most of whom already offer CATS (Credit Accumulation and Transfer Scheme), modular courses and programmes that make studying abroad infinitely more straightforward, such as Erasmus (see glossary).

The New Universities – shown as ☐ in the tables
These used to be polytechnics or institutes before 1992. Although they may occupy just one site, they are often the product of several

colleges and are spread across a number of campuses. They form a separate group because they still hold true to the original polytechnic doctrine of vocational courses and strong ties with industry – typically through placements and work experience. As a student you're likely to have an increased number of contact hours here, but not necessarily a greater workload. And generally the transition from poly to uni happened a bit quickly to cope with the surge of extra students, so there is considerable stress on resources and facilities. Despite their new name, they still suffer discrimination, and many employers honestly believe that a degree from here 'isn't as good' as one from the Old Universities! The New Universities tend to be more flexible about what type of qualifications you need to get in. And they have a better name than the Old Universities for pastoral care. This refers to the relationship between staff and students. The idea being that giving each student a personal tutor – an ear for all academic and social grievances – makes for an easier time at university. The fact that your tutor has a number of other students to listen to, other work, may not be available when you need them and won't insist that you visit them anyway, mean that what is a great idea on paper, doesn't always deliver in practice.

The Colleges – shown as ⌘ in the tables

Usually these are specialist institutions and consequently provide excellent facilities in their chosen fields despite their size. They are sometimes affiliated to universities eg Holborn College and the University of Wolverhampton. This form of franchising means the college buys the right to teach the degree, which the university will award, providing that the course meets the standards set by the university.

A summary of the differences between old universities, new universities and colleges

Old Universities	New Universities	Colleges
Generally single site campuses	Usually multisite, commonly in urban areas	Smaller than the universities
More bias towards tutorials and seminars	Teaching contact time generally higher	Specialist courses often renowned e.g. The LSE

23

Old Universities	New Universities	Colleges
More likely to be 100% exam assessed	More likely to have continuous assessment as well as exams	Often have excellent facilities
Strengths in teaching and research	Traditionally have closer liaison with industry	Sometimes have specific links with industry

Structure

A campus is a purpose-built site where all the teaching facilities and student accommodation are on a single site. Multisite institutions are those where the teaching facilitites are at several different and often distant locations.

This table summarises the main differences between campus and multisite universities:

Campus	Multisite
Generally campus universities are out of town	Individual sites are usually more centrally located in towns and cities
Friendly university community	May lack a community atmosphere
Often active Student Union	Students' Union activities less accessible
Good range of on-site facilities (shops, banks, eating places)	More convenient for day-to-day living : food shopping, wide range of banks etc.
Easy access to whole university, socialising with other faculties	Often rely on non-university amenities
Can feel claustrophobic and isolated	Easier to get out of the university environment if you want to
Age and range of people generally narrower than in normal communities	Usually closer to non-university community

Below are the 7 possible combinations you can choose from. Look at them and then fill in Question 2 in the Questionnaire.

●◆	Old Uni – campus
●❖	Old Uni – multisite
☐◆	New Uni – campus
☐❖	New Uni – multisite
✠❖	Poly – multisite
✠◆	College etc. – campus
✠❖	College etc. – multisite

Now enter your decision in section 2 of the questionnaire on page 64.

☐ HOW EMPLOYABLE WILL YOU BE AT THE END OF THE COURSE?

You'll almost certainly be bearing in mind how employable you'll be when you choose which course and at which institution to apply for.

The fifth column in the tables, headed employment, ranks the universities from the best (1) to the worst (97) in terms of their graduate employment record. The information is based on the comprehensive tables in *The Times Good University Guide 1994-1995*.

You'll also notice a column headed 'value added' – column four. This too is a ranking based on information in the Times guide. Value added is supposed to show the extent to which universities have added value to their students by having accepted them in the first place and then overseen their university careers. Entry qualifications of entrants are related to an exit measure which is constructed from a combination of degree completion rates, firsts and employment figures. The ranking here should be taken lightly – the figures on which it is based are not standardised and therfore not strictly comparable. They might, however, help you choose between two similar institutions.

Always remember that your employability is dependent on your final degree result and on your personal skills and motivations. If you want to maximise your choice in the job market you should work hard to get the best possible results.

☐ WHAT KIND OF COURSE ARE YOU AFTER?

You know how you want to be taught, but what about course content? The degree subject column tells you what courses are available and what subjects you can study with your Accountancy, Business Studies or Economics choice. Do you want to study a subject on its own (a Single Honours degree), with another subject (Joint or Combined degree) or as part of a modular programme alongside a multitude of subject areas?

Single Honours courses are shown by an S in the *degree type* column and Combined/Joint Honours courses by a J in the *degree type* column.

A diagram showing some of the many different types of courses available

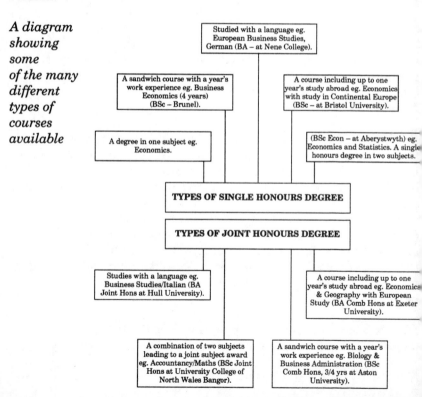

Studied with a language eg. European Business Studies, German (BA – at Nene College).

A sandwich course with a year's work experience eg. Business Economics (4 years) (BSc – Brunel).

A course including up to one year's study abroad eg. Economics with study in Continental Europe (BSc – at Bristol University).

A degree in one subject eg. Economics.

(BSc Econ – at Aberystwyth) eg. Economics and Statistics. A single honours degree in two subjects.

TYPES OF SINGLE HONOURS DEGREE

TYPES OF JOINT HONOURS DEGREE

Studies with a language eg. Business Studies/Italian (BA Joint Hons at Hull University).

A course including up to one year's study abroad eg. Economics & Geography with European Study (BA Comb Hons at Exeter University).

A combination of two subjects leading to a joint subject award eg. Accountancy/Maths (BSc Joint Hons at University College of North Wales Bangor).

A sandwich course with a year's work experience eg. Biology & Business Administration (BSc Comb Hons, 3/4 yrs at Aston University).

If a **Single Honours** course sounds interesting, bear in mind that a good range of optional subjects might make it even more inviting. You don't want to be stuck with just a handful of choices from which to fill in your timetable after you've put down the core courses. Options may be related to your own subject or from a completely different discipline. Some universities and colleges can only offer a limited selection, whilst others provide courses from separate faculties and even separate universities. Modular degrees usually have a wide range of subjects and students have an unrestricted choice barring timetable clashes.

Alternatively, if you feel a compulsion to specialise in just one other area, then a Joint degree might be more up your street. Some **Joint degrees** do not require previous knowledge of the second subject. Others, especially those with a European language often specify that candidates must have an A-level or GCSE level for background knowledge. With Joint degrees, be wary of courses that have seemingly identical titles, for example, Business Studies with German, Business Studies and German and Business Studies and German Business. In the first one, Business Studies is the major subject; in the second, you'll probably spend equal time on each and in the third the stress is on German Business rather than German language. Any of them may involve some time abroad.

Sandwich Courses involve taking time out from the lecture theatre to gain work experience relevant to the degree. This should give you a competitive advantage on graduation – you'll have experience and a referee; you may even de offered employment after graduation by the company who you work for during the sandwich period. On the minus side, sandwich courses generally mean that you'll graduate after four years rather than after three.

Studying overseas could be another factor in the race to narrow down your choices. Not all of these courses however will make you pack your bags for a full year. Neither must you be a linguist, since you can study overseas in English in, for example, North America and the Netherlands.

COURSE COMBINATIONS – HOW THEY'RE SHOWN IN THE TABLES
Where the course title is two subjects the titles are written to show which of the two subjects is the major one – or whether both subjects are studied equally.

Usually the subject written first is the main subject. Sometimes the first subject or the combination of subjects will indicate the bias of the course – whether it will lead to a BSc, a BA, or a Social Science degree (BSocSc).

e.g.

BSc – BUSINESS ECONOMICS (University of East London)
BA – ECONOMICS (Manchester Metropolitan University)
BA – ECONOMICS & CHEMISTRY (Manchester Metropolitan University)
BSocSc – ECONOMICS & POLITICS (Keele)

The list below shows what the abbreviations used in the tables mean:

ECON & GEOG	Economics and Geography
ACC – ECON	Accountancy and Economics
PSY/BA	Psychology and Business Administration
BS **WITH** SOC	Business Studies with Sociology
BUS **(& 23 COMB OPT) 13**	Business and a choice of 23 Modular/Combined Options

Where possible the length of the course, entry requirements, and whether the course is new or not are specified in the table if all the options available have the same details. Where some course options are of different lengths or have different entrance requirements, these differences are specified in brackets beside the option details given in *Additional Information*,which follows the tables. For example, in *Additional Information* number 13 is Anglia Polytechnic University. Go to the list under the heading Business Studies and find number 13.

13   ANGLIA PO/U
Bus/Soc. Pol, (3yrs,12,New); Comm St (3yrs,14); Chem, Maths, RT Comput Sys (3 yrs, 8); Instrum Elect (3yrs, 8, New); Geol (10, New); Eur Thou & Lit (12); Contem Eur St, Geog, Graph Art, Hist, Art Hist, Music, Polit, Soc, Wom St, (3yrs,14), Fr, Ger, Ital, Span (4yrs,14) Law (16).

The information in brackets gives specific details about some of the options:

Option described as	Description means
Bus/Soc Pol(3 yrs)...	3 years study
Bus/Geol(New)....	New course available this year
Bus/Law(16)....	Entry requirement is 16 points

Now go to the questionnaire on page 64 and fill in your answers to questions three and four. Then work your way through the table for your main subject and put a line through the courses left uncrossed if they've got the wrong combinations or content for you.

☐ QUALIFICATION GAINED

BSc, BA, BCom, BSoc Sci, BEng ... the list goes on and on. This, however, is not a good basis upon which to select the course, but gives an indication of the bias of the course content. You'll see some qualification names crop up here and there as you work through the subject choices in column 5 and 6.

In Column 8, you will see two options

DEG   Degree
HND   Higher National Diploma

The majority of the courses are degrees, but most of the 2 year courses will be HNDs. Degrees generally take 3-5 years, although there are a few places that offer degree courses in 2 years with different term schedules. If you are interested, check the details with the university.

Now go to Question 5 of the questionnaire and fill in your qualification preference, if you have one.

☐ COURSE DURATION

Course duration is shown in the eighth and ninth column of the tables. The Full-time study, in the column headed duration, ranges from 1 to 4 years. Sandwich courses, in the column headed S, last from 2 to 5 years. University of the West of England (UWE), Bristol, Buckinghamshire College and Cardiff Institute offer a 1 year degree course. Before you get excited and think you can be out earning lots of money in 1 short year, note that these are 1 year courses to convert HNDs to degrees. So, generally, Hons degrees are 3 or 4 years, the extra year being spent studying abroad or gaining work experience in the UK, Europe or North America. For some courses the additional year is a compulsory component, for others you can elect whether to add a year of work/study abroad or not. Itís really a case of personal preference and you have to balance the benefits of gaining valuable work/research experience against the possible financial strain that the extra year will incur. If you get paid during your year out you'll need to return to the frugal lifestyle of a student if you are to make ends meet.

Now fill in the length of course you prefer in Question 6 of the questionnaire.

☐ WILL YOUR A-LEVELS BE GOOD ENOUGH?

Obviously, for the majority of students, their A-level scores will be the decisive means of natural selection. And it's important to be honest about the grades you're heading for. Don't be too pessimistic but, on the other hand, there's no point in kidding yourself about your as yet undiscovered genius. Talk to your teachers for an accurate picture of your predicted grades.

The *subjects required* column shows specific subjects needed to satisfy the entry requirements for that particular course, usually Maths, a Language or a Science. The *grades required* column lists the grades or points required for entry into the course. A certain amount of bargaining is possible for first time applicants, but should never be relied upon.

‡ or ▲ in either of the columns means that you need to check the prospectus or with the institution for specific requirements. Where there are no subjects, grades or points specified you need to find out what the university is looking for. Sometimes they like to keep their options open and sometimes their offers are too diverse to allow

them to be specific on what is required. **L** means a language is required, **Sc** a science, **+** or **£** – Maths or Economics.

HOW TO COUNT YOUR UCAS POINTS

A-levels		AS-levels		BTEC
A	10	A	5	If you are doing BTEC courses put an M for an expected Merit result and a D for a Distinction and check with the university about the requirements.
B	8	B	4	
C	6	C	3	
D	4	D	2	
E	2	E	1	
Note 1: If you're taking 4 A-levels only count your best 3. **Note 2**: Do not count General Studies.		**Note:** Most places like you to have done 2 AS-levels for every A-level that they request. This is to show that you can cope with the workload of a degree course.		

The grades listed in the quick reference table are just for GCE A-levels, but many universities will accept other equivalent qualifications, such as BTEC or GNVQ and Scottish and Irish Highers. Some places specify particular grades but will still take you on if you get the same point score. So, for example, if you are supposed to get ABC (which amounts to 10+8+6 = 24 points), then any combination which produces 24 points (ie BBB or AAD) may be OK. Few courses specify subjects they want you to have studied (with the exception of most European languages Joint degrees which demand you know at least a bit of the relevant language). Conversely, other universities will adamantly reject A-levels like General Studies, or the less academic ones such as Art, whilst 'traditional' qualifications are welcomed everywhere.

Now go to Question 7 on the questionnaire and write down:

1) The subjects you are taking
2) The level of exam (A, AS, BTEC)
3) Your predicted grades
4) The points equivalent of the grades

Also, note that there are many courses in the tables that don't specify grades. You will need to talk to the department in that university to find out what is required and if you're eligible.

There are alternative qualifications such as Scottish and Irish exams. There is not enough space here to include all possible combinations of acceptable entry qualifications, so you should ask the university directly. Bearing all this in mind, go back to the grades required column, and carry on your selection process. Cross off all the places that ask for a score which is more than four points above your total. The extra points have been added to give some leeway.

☐ STATISTICS

The *statistics* columns, headed entry /apply, /get on and /% – are mainly for information – to give you an idea of the recent number of students applying for courses and the numbers accepted.

e.g.
APPLY: Number of students applying for the course 2269
GET ON: Number of students accepted for the course 334
%:   Number of acceptances to applications expressed as
           a percentage 15%

These figures give you an idea (where the statistics are available) about how popular the course is and how likely you are to get on to the course.

One final point – where you see the word NEW, this means that the course is new this year. There are 9 new Accountancy courses, 44 new Business Studies courses and 28 new Economics courses, 81 new courses in these three subjects this year. Remember that these courses haven't been tried or tested. While they are potentially exciting, you'll be the guinea pigs. Expect some settling down time as the course becomes established.

☐ QUALITY OF TEACHING

Another factor that could influence your choice of course could be the quality of teaching.

The system for ranking UK Universities in order of teaching quality is in its infancy and, for the time being, you will have to rely on the quality of research.

Strength in research is usually regarded as an indication of the quality of a department at an institution. Departments with research strengths are also likely to possess staff with the qualities that are important for teaching.

Accountancy
Aberystwyth, Bristol, Edinburgh, Essex, Exeter, Leeds, London (LSE), Manchester, Strathclyde and Thames Valley.

Business Studies
Bradford, Cardiff, City, Lancaster, London (LSE), Southampton, Strathclyde, UMIST, and Warwick.

Economics
Aberdeen, Birmingham, Bristol, Cambridge, East Anglia, Essex, Exeter, Glasgow, Liverpool, London (LSE) (UC) (QMW), Newcastle, Nottingham, Oxford, Reading, Southampton, Stirling, Strathclyde, Sussex, Swansea, Warwick and York.

☐ NARROWING THE CHOICE

Now you should be in a position to use the answers in your questionnaire to go through the tables crossing out all courses which do not meet the criteria you have set yourself. You should be left with about 15 combinations of university and course. If not, go back over your answers and try to narrow the choice.

☐ CHECKLIST

Check that you have thought about everything on the checklist below and when you can honestly answer 'Yes, I've given it some serious consideration' then tick off the box.

Have you given serious consideration to ....

Where you want to study – which areas?	
The type of place you want to study at – old or new?	
Whether you want a campus or non campus university	
The teaching and assessment methods and quality	
How long you want to study for	
Your predicted grades	
Your employability after graduation	
The qualification you'll gain at the end of the course	
How likely you are to get on to the course	

Now it's up to you, but I can offer you one last PLAN of action:

Prospectus – get one for each place you are thinking of applying to

Look again at whether your needs are met by this place

Arrange to visit and get a feel for the place

Narrow down your choices to a maximum of eight, use the preference chart in Section C to rank your choices in order of preference then fill in your UCAS form and send it off.

Good Luck!

Chapter 5
COMPLETING YOUR UCAS FORM

General advice on filling in your UCAS form is given in another guide in this series, *How to Complete Your UCAS Form*, co-written by Dr Tony Higgins, Chief Executive of UCAS. (See Reading List)

The following advice is directed at helping you complete section 10, your personal statement. This is your opportunity to explain to the university admissions staff why you want to study Accountancy, Business Studies or Economics.

☐ FILLING IN YOUR PERSONAL SECTION

The personal section of the UCAS form is the only chance you get to recommend yourself as a serious candidate worthy of a place, or at least, worthy of an interview. It is therefore vital that you think very carefully indeed about how to complete it so that it shows you in the best possible light. You must sell yourself and make it hard for them not to take you.

Obviously, there are as many ways of completing your section 10 as there are candidates. There are no rules as such, but there are recommendations that can be made.

Universities are academic institutions and thus you must present yourself as a strong academic bet. The first thing that the admissions tutor reading your form wants to know is the strength of your commitment to academic study. Say clearly why you wish to study. Money, status, family traditions, the sound of your own voice etc. are not good reasons. Give details and examples of what precisely it is about the subject that interests you, referring to recent news items, and debates. Explain what you hope to get out of three years of academic study. Tell the admissions tutor what related material you have recently read and explain why you appreciated it.

Work experience is useful as it demonstrates a commitment to the subject outside the classroom. If you have had relevant work experience talk about it on your form. Explain concisely what your job entailed.

Future plans can also be included on your form, if you have any. Be precise. Again this will demonstrate a breadth of interest in the subject.

At least half of your section 10 should deal with material directly related to your chosen course. Thereafter, use the rest of the page – you must use it all – to tell the admissions tutor what makes you who you are. What travel have you undertaken? What do you read? What sporting achievements do you have? What music do you like or play? In all these things give details. This...

> *Last year I went to France. I like reading and listening to music and sometimes I play football at weekends.*

...is weak. A stronger version could read,

> *Last year I went to Paris and visited all the Impressionist galleries there. I relax by reading American short stories – Andre Dubus, Raymond Carver amongst others. My musical taste is largely focused on opera (I have seen 14 productions of 'The Magic Flute') and I would like to continue playing the 'cello in an orchestra at university. I would also enjoy the chance to play in a football team to keep myself fit.*

Make them want to teach you; make them want to meet you.

Chapter 6
SUCCEEDING IN YOUR INTERVIEW

Outside Oxford and Cambridge and applications for certain courses, such as medicine, formal interviews are rarely part of the admissions process. They are expensive and time consuming for both the university and the applicants. Nevertheless, our research shows that sixth-formers do worry about interviews and we wanted to include advice on them in this guide.

Also, it's worth bearing in mind that if you shine in your interview and impress the admissions staff no end, then they may drop their grades slightly and make you a lower offer in the hope that you will join them, even if you slip a couple of points in your exams.

Every interview is a character-building experience and need not be as daunting as most candidates fear. There are a number of practical steps that can be taken to reduce the anxiety that inevitably occurs when strangers ask you demanding questions.

While the number of people conducting the interview and the length of time it takes can vary, all interviews are designed to enable those asking the questions to find out as much about the candidate as they can. It is important, therefore, to engage actively with the process (good eye-contact and confident body language help here) and view it as a chance to put yourself across rather than as an obstacle course designed to catch you out.

Interviewers are more interested in what you know than what you do not. If you are asked a question to which you do not know the answer, say so. To waffle (or worse, to lie) simply wastes time and lets you down. The interviewers will be considering the quality of thought that goes into your answers; they will not expect you to know everything already. Pauses while you think are completely acceptable; do not be afraid to take your time.

It is important to remember that there is a strong chance that amongst the people interviewing you will be those who actually tutor you during your time at university. Enthusiasm for, and a strong commitment to your subject and, above all, a willingness to learn are thus extremely important attitudes to convey. The people you meet at interview not only have to judge your academic calibre but also have to evaluate whether they would enjoy teaching you for the next three or four years.

An ability to think on your feet is vital. Pre-learned answers never work; they appear glib and superficial and no matter how apparently spontaneously they are delivered, they are always detectable. Putting forward an answer step by step, using examples and factual knowledge to reinforce your points will impress interviewers far more, even if you are uncertain of what you say. Obviously, this is especially true for candidates wishing to read literary subjects, but the general principle applies across the board. That said, it is also sensible to admit defeat if your argument is demolished. Being gracious in defeat signifies not only intelligence – knowing that you have been beaten – but also a level of maturity.

It is possible to steer the interview yourself to some extent. If, for example, you are asked about something about which you know nothing, confidently replacing that question with another related one yourself shows enthusiasm. (This requires a bit of care however, since you don't want to appear arrogant coming to an interview and supplying your own questions!) It is important that time is not wasted in silences that are as embarrassing for the interviewer as for the candidate.

Essential preparation includes revision of the personal section of your UCAS form – this document may well form the basis of preliminary questions. It is not therefore wise to include anything on your form about which you are unprepared to speak.

Questions may well be asked on your extra-curricular activities. Most often, this is a tactic designed to put you at your ease and therefore your answers should be thorough and enthusiastic but you should avoid spending too long over them.

At the end of the interview, those conducting it may well ask if there is anything you would like to ask them. If there is nothing, then say that your interview has covered all that you had thought of. It is sensible though, to have one or two questions of a serious kind – to do with the course, the tuition and so on – up your sleeve. It is not wise, obviously, to ask them anything that you could and should have found out from the prospectus. It is also permissible and even desirable to ask a question based on the conversations that have made up the interview. This marks you out as someone who listens, is curious and who is willing to learn.

Above all, make them remember you when they go through a list of twenty or more candidates at the end of the day.

☐ PREPARATION FOR AN ACCOUNTANCY, BUSINESS STUDIES OR ECONOMICS INTERVIEW

Preparation for an interview should be an intensification of the work you are already doing outside class for your A-level courses. Interviewers will be looking for evidence of an academic interest and commitment that extends beyond the classroom. They will also be looking for an ability to apply the theories and methods that you have been learning in your A-level courses to the real world.

Newspapers and Magazines

As an A-level student, you should already be reading a quality newspaper every day and at the weekends. Before your interview it is vital that you are aware of current affairs related to the course for which you are being interviewed. The best weekend papers to read are:

• The Weekend *Financial Times*,
• The Saturday and Sunday *Telegraph*,
• The Saturday and Sunday *Times*.

You need obviously to pay particular attention to the Business Sections of these papers.

Magazines are another important source of comment on current issues and deeper analysis. *The Economist* is the most reliable example but you may also find it helpful to pick up the more specialist magazines such as *Business Age* or *Accountancy Age*.

Reading professionally-written articles both keeps you well-informed of relevant current events and gives you the chance to see how the professional writers use the vocabulary and language of business to communicate the news and their views.

Television and Radio

It is also important to watch or listen to the news every day, again paying particular attention to business news and economic news. Documentaries and programmes about the economy, business ventures, the politics of business (privatisation, taxation etc.) and so on can be enormously helpful in showing how what you are studying is applied to actual situations and events. The 'Money Programme' is a good example of the sort of television programme it would be useful to watch.

Radio Four has its equivalent in 'Money Box' and 'The Today Programme' in the morning has up-to-the-minute reporting on economic and business developments, often with interviews given by those most closely involved.

It is a good idea to know who the Chairman of the CBI and the Chairman the Bank of England are, for example, and the names of the country's top business men and women. You can then make a point of listening to what they have to say when they appear on 'Question Time' on TV, 'Any Question' on the radio or are interviewed on 'Newsnight'.

Interview Questions

Interview questions are likely to test your knowledge of business and economic events and developments in the real world. Any controversial related topics could well be brought up by interviewers and it is important that you are well informed enough to have an opinion about them from a business or economic point of view. Recent examples of such topics might be privatisation, EuroDisney, the Channel Tunnel or what it means to be part of Europe.

It is important that your answers are delivered in appropriate language. You will impress interviewers with fluent use of precise, technical terms and thus detailed knowledge of the definitions of business and economic words and phrases is essential.

You might be asked what parts of the A-level courses you have most enjoyed. You need, therefore, to think carefully about this before interview and, if possible, steer the interview in the direction of these topics so that you can display your knowledge.

Future plans and possible careers may also be discussed at interview. You will not be expected to have made up your mind about this absolutely, but by the same token, you will not be held to what you say at interview after you have left university. Previous work experience is useful, and in this respect, it is important to recall the precise tasks you carried out during your employment and think about them before interview so that you can answer questions on them fully and well if they come up. Questions of this kind will be asked to see if you have an understanding of how theories and methods are actually applied in the world outside school or college.

Chapter 7
CURRENT ISSUES

☐ ACCOUNTANCY

The world of accountancy is dynamic and varied. Whichever area of
work you decide to go into, there will always be current issues and
controversies. These range from technical issues to business issues,
from small local problems to problems with international
implications.

Spectacular Company Collapses

Over recent years, particularly during the recession, there has been
a stream of spectacular company collapses and disasters – BCCI,
Polly Peck, Queen's Moat Houses and the Maxwell empire to name
but a few. Accountants from many firms and disciplines are involved
in these affairs. Several are from the insolvency areas trying to
rescue parts of the business (as they did with the successful sale of
Mirror Group Newspapers), others are concentrating on trying to
trace missing assets and funds into complex trusts and offshore
companies throughout the world. This is often painstaking work, but
ultimately very satisfying when the complex webs are untangled.

One also finds accountant pitted against accountant in lengthy and
complicated litigation: this is because accountants from different
firms will be working for each side in any dispute. For example, the
auditors of a failed conglomerate such as Polly Peck could well find
themselves being sued by the receivers and liquidators of one or
more parts of the business. You can read some more about this in the
Queen's Moat House case study later on in this chapter.

Company collapses and insolvencies provide all disciplines, from the
investigative and sometimes dangerous work of the insolvency
practitioners to the legal and technical work required to bring and
defend actions in court, with opportunities to develop their skills and
gain greater experience.

F.R.S. 3

The communication of company information through the accounts has been the subject of much debate recently. The introduction of FRS 3 (Financial Reporting Standard) has radically changed the way financial performance is reported to enable shareholders and others to get a better appreciation of where a group's profits and losses are coming from. FRS 3 is but one part of an ambitious programme to change the nature of financial reporting and to eliminate as far as possible the 'creative' use of accounting techniques to portray an unrepresentative picture of a group's financial position. Whether you are poacher or gamekeeper, whether you are an accountant in industry trying to use the regulations to your best advantage or whether you are involved in the standard setting and monitoring procedures, these are exciting current areas in which to be involved.

The Cadbury Report

Other current issues include the Cadbury Report which seeks to reshape the composition of the boards of directors for plcs. Accountants will be involved in advising boards on their structure, and some will become board members in non-executive and executive capacities. The relationship between auditors and the boards of public companies is also set to change. The Cadbury Report recommends the creation of audit committees comprising at least three non-executive directors to meet and liaise with the auditors on a regular basis.

In conclusion, we live in an exciting and ever changing world. Business has become a global affair, and the need for techniques, practices and regulations to facilitate and monitor these changes is very much in the sphere of the accountant. There are always current issues to deal with no matter which branch of accountancy you choose to specialise in.

☐ BUSINESS

If you ask someone in business what they see as the current issues, you'll most likely get a reply like 'our overdraft' or 'the way the bank's treating us' or 'whether our debtors will pay up before we go under'. These are always areas of concern.

Taking a more general view, with the recession appearing to be coming to an end, issues other than its depth or length are emerging. People can see the 'green shoots' emerging and are turning their attention to how to nurture the crop, how to protect it from the pests of inflation and excessive legislation. Business people want to see the burden imposed by the government, in the form of direct and indirect taxation, reduced.

If you look at other current issues, then five main strands emerge: inflation and pay, competitiveness, the greening of business, Europe and, finally, deregulation.

Inflation and pay

Inflation has been reduced by strict monetarist policies – control of public spending. As we emerge from recession there is a danger that inflation will rise. Businesses are concerned that it is kept under control - fundamentally by the government controlling pay in the public sector. This will not only set an example for the private sector but also will help to balance the budget and pay, perhaps, for further tax cuts – so encouraging spending.

Increases in wages paid by business don't only threaten inflation. They also counteract cost-cutting policies. It is becoming increasingly uncommon for employees to receive an annual increment to their pay packets. Pay is linked to increases in productivity rather than to maintaining employees' purchasing power. New, formalised pay agreements are being drawn up which introduce profit-related and performance-related pay into new areas of the private sector. Tax incentives, introduced by the government to encourage such schemes, have made it advantageous for employees to take up the schemes. By such formal links between profitability and pay it is hoped that the scope for inflation will be reduced.

Competitiveness

Many business people, particularly those working internationally, see one of the most important issues as gauging and improving the UK's competitiveness in world markets. There is no doubt that UK businesses are unable to compete effectively with the emerging economies of what is termed The Third World or those of Eastern Europe in terms of cost. This is not to say that cost reduction isn't vital.

Businesses are increasingly being forced to concentrate on what is termed *value added*. To win orders the important factors are quality, service and aftercare. We may not produce the cheapest cars or clothing or electronic goods so we must produce the best.

To beat the competition in a value added market businesses need access to a workforce that can add value. Skills training and the educational standards of the workforce are an area in which the UK is not competitive with other countries in European and world markets. Enrolment in higher and postgraduate education is increasing and standards of teaching and the ways in which these standards are monitored are improving. Yet we are competing with countries like South Korea where one electronics company employs over 1000 people who have completed PhDs. To be competitive within the market, employees need to maximise their skills portfolio.

By concentrating on adding value and on promoting training UK businesses will be able to increase their competitiveness.

The greening of business

Every business creates waste. Every business is affected by 'green' legislation aimed at reducing waste and at controlling pollution.

As mentioned in the next chapter (Current Issues in Economics), the government is introducing or proposing to introduce economic instruments in line with the principle of 'polluter pays'. Because of these, businesses are having to cope with increased costs: increased taxes on road transport, increased costs of water and electricity to pay for improvements to water and air quality. Moreover, these costs are now variable – i.e. costs which were once annual payments – water rates, for example, are increasingly likely to vary in proportion to usage. Businesses will pay per volume of effluent discharged rather than a flat annual rate.

In addition to green legislation there are important legal precedents to be clarified. The most far-reaching of these is to do with the costs of cleaning up contaminated land which, as 'polluter pays' suggests, is to be paid for by the person or company who caused the land to become contaminated.

As you're no doubt aware, companies are frequently taken over, sites frequently change hands. When this happens, who should pay the cost of decontaminating the site? Should it be the current owner or the person who contaminated the land? What if the company that caused the contamination has ceased to exist? Who benefits from the site being decontaminated? These legal aspects remain to be sorted out. When they are, several businesses could find themselves with large liabilities for the costs of decontamination.

Europe

'The corner that we fight from, whether we like it or not, is the EC.'

Open barriers allow a two-way flow of goods and services. As a nation we must export more than we import to achieve long-term economic growth. As the EC coheres businesses will increasingly see European countries, whether they like it or not, as an internal market. Exports will be to countries outside the EC.

As mentioned previously, under the heading of competitiveness, the UK lags behind most of the rest of Europe in skills training and workforce education. While we do not subscribe to the Social Chapter of the Maastricht Treaty its influence will still be felt.

The influence of Brussels will become more pervasive. At the time of writing one of the major issues to concern businesses are the EC directives on waste and product packaging. While it may be laudable to seek to reduce wastage, to conserve resources by restricting packaging and by stipulating recyclability requirements of packaging, such measures are often costly for businesses to implement. In addition to changing manufacturing and packaging processes business will have to accept that attention will be increasingly focused on the product rather than the packaging.

With the opening up of new markets for business in the EC, with its expansion to include not only EFTA countries but also the emerging companies of Eastern Europe, avenues will be created along which businesses will be able to expand. What is clear is that Europe as an issue won't go away. It isn't a case of 'love it or leave it'. We are a part of Europe and, as such, must accept the benefits this offers and cope with the restriction it imposes.

Deregulation

The government is trying to reduce the amount of legislation that affects business. Compliance with legislation costs businesses a great deal of time and in many cases money where professional services must be paid for to ensure compliance. The government has abolished the statutory annual audit for small companies and is continually raising the threshold for compulsory VAT registration. In other areas legislation is being codified and simplified to make it easier to run a business.

Big Companies' Bully Tactics

Many small companies find it hard to get their hands on money owed to them by big companies. During the recession this has been argued to be the cause of a significant proportion of company failures. As a country the UK has the most extended credit terms of any in Europe. Small businesses have immense problems in controlling cashflows, big companies benefit from holding onto cash until the last possible moment. The small companies have no option but to accept this behaviour by applying for the contracts offered by the big companies or do no business

Banks and their behaviour

Banks have been criticised for their overbearing behaviour towards companies, for levying excessive charges and for behaving as if they owned the businesses. Compared with other countries in Europe, particularly Germany, banks in the UK have little involvement in the day to day running of business and operate what is often seen as almost a protection racket. In Germany banks often take equity stakes in the companies they lend money to. In the UK banks take charges over company assets. This, combined with the fact that many banks are affected by the needs of the stock markets to show high levels of profitability has led to over-prudent behaviour and accusations that, at the first signs of trouble banks have pulled the plug on several business to protect their investments in the short term when a better long-term solution would have been to steward the business through its hard times and to benefit from the increased charges it would be able to make in the future from a successful business.

☐ ECONOMICS

Green Economics

As awareness of environmental damage has increased, economists have attempted to develop ways of evaluating the damage and have been at the forefront of investigating 'polluter pays' policies. These policies start from the premise that the environment is a scarce resource and that it is equitable that people pay in proportion to their use of this resource.

The question 'Why is there litter in the public park but no litter in my back garden?' is a lay expression of disquiet with the way the economic system worked until recently. In a report on the UK economy published in January 1993 the O.E.C.D. (Organisation for Economic Co-operation and Development) states:

'Open access to environmental resources implies that they may be regarded by economic agents as common property, and that the full costs of environmental damage are not taken into account in individual decisions.'

A number of market-based economic instruments have been introduced to rebalance matters. The principal of these are:

- User's charges: industrial effluent charged for on volume, rather than a flat rate

- Household waste recycling credits : payments by local authorities to recyclers reflecting savings in disposal/collection costs by authorities

- Petrol taxes increased

- The introduction of road pricing and toll motorways

- Increased registration fees for heavy lorries – to compensate for the extra damage they do to roads

The development of a distinct brand of 'green economics' is likely to continue as the politicians are pressurised to react to increasing environmental degradation.

The opening up of Eastern Europe

The liberalisation of economic systems in states formerly under the influence of the Soviet Union has had a dramatic effect on those countries.

Most smaller enterprises, once under state control, have now been privatised. The transformation and privatisation of larger enterprises has proved more difficult than anticipated – particularly in Hungary and Poland. A combination of political and budgetary pressures threaten the attainment of satisfactory growth in the medium-term.

Most of the former Eastern Bloc countries are experiencing problems of high inflation and political unease. Recent elections in Hungary have shown that a large proportion of the voting population, bewildered by freedom and choice, hanker for a return to the days of regulation and false stability. In all of the newly-industrialising states the vital need is for access to foreign markets and for investments of foreign currency.

The situation in these countries at the moment is exciting. There is still a need for further economic reform if long-term growth is to be achieved. The major question to be answered seems to be one of how far and how fast the populations of these countries will allow reforms to take place.

Privatisation

The result of a combination of anti-collectivist political ideals, liberal economic thought and, in many cases, of a need to balance budgets, privatisation has been one of the major economic events of the past decade. From a slightly hesitant start in the UK in the early 1980s privatisation is now a major global phenomenon. In most of the remaining areas of the economy still in public hands we are seeing 'Son of Privatisation' in the form of the widespread introduction of Compulsory Competitive Tendering.

Recently, however, some commentators have questioned the extent to which privatisation has succeeded. While the answer to such questions must depend largely on how one views the objectives of the policy – whether political or economic, many people are wondering whether, in many cases, private monopolies have simply replaced public ones. Have inefficiencies actually been reduced? How free from state control are the now-private companies?

Neil Clarke the Chairman of British Coal – one of the last remaining state-owned companies in the UK – has recently said:

'Preconceptions are widely held. Apparently nationalised industries are old fashioned, bureaucratic, unwilling to change, unenterprising. This is completely wrong. The people here are technically extremely able. Very hard driving. Very willing to change. These preconceptions are widely held and wrongly held.'

He continues, saying that the problem with nationalised industries is that governments have always insisted on interfering in their running.

The main area of debate for economists is one of what modifications are needed to the regulatory framework for privatised firms so that profits are achieved through efficiency gains and not from exploitation of market power.

It is likely that government policies all over the world will see greater use being made of freed market mechanisms generally and specifically of policies of privatisation.

Economists will need to discover and decide what mechanisms to put in place to ensure that the newly privatised enterprises face the same need to make profits from efficiency gains as the other enterprises in the market.

Some other current issues:
- Education and training reform
- Labour market flexibility
- Benefit-related employment traps

APPENDIX

In this section we give information on the recruiting practices of several well-known companies.

☐ ACCOUNTANCY

Stoy Hayward takes about 100 students (ie trainee accountants) each year. Many have degrees in business related subjects but many do not. The firm does not set out to recruit students with 'relevant' degrees – but obviously, students from such courses are often attracted to accountancy. Stoys deliberately looks for a mixture of applicants. It wants people with varied backgrounds, personalities and interest rather than 'clones'.

Students should have taken a degree for enjoyment – and achieved. ('It's better to have a 2:1 in English than a pass in something else'.) They should also have 18 UCAS points at A-level.

Numeracy is important. It is tested for at interview. So equally is communication skill, both verbal and written. The firm says that students do not always realise how much time they will spend in explaining matters to clients or in composing letters and reports. The second interview stage takes one day and includes numeracy and abstract reasoning tests.

Stoy Haywards' clients are smaller than those of many accountancy firms. Students therefore spend two to three weeks on assignment rather than three months. They must be adaptable, good at establishing relationships quickly, and confident. The firm places great stress on personal qualities. It is, therefore, important to be able to show evidence of initiative, of the ability to communicate and work in a team – through membership of societies, voluntary work, independent travel in vacations etc.

1994 starting salary – £16,000 plus a bonus after 10 months which brings the total to £17,000. (London figures. Less in the provinces.)

Ernst and Young also state no preference for particular subjects*. They have not found that accountancy graduates perform significantly better in professional examinations. About 17 per cent of recruits annually have accountancy degrees: the remainder come from a wide variety of subjects.

What does the firm insist on? A 2.2 is the minimum degree class. A 2.1 is preferred and the majority of recruits have one. A-level grades are extremely important – applicants must have a minimum of 22 UCAS points (eg BBC) – and a grade B in GCSE maths. Languages are beneficial, but preference would not be given to linguists without the other skills Ernst & Young seek. These are amongst others: a positive attitude, a professional demeanour, team skills, the ability to deliver practical solutions as well as numerical skills. All of these are tested during the selection process. The firm is looking for people who are actively involved in extra-curricular activities and who can demonstrate that they possess the commitment and motivation to succeed in a competitive environment.

Ernst & Young participate in the milkround at over 30 universities but increasingly find that students choose to apply directly to the firm in advance of the milkround. They also run an extensive programme of campus events for first and second year undergraduates at universities throughout the UK.

Starting salary for the London office in autumn 1994 was £16,000 with profit-related pay.

(*They did stress that this may not be the pattern in their provincial offices which do their own recruitment.)

Price Waterhouse had a target intake of approximately 450 students in 1994, the majority to train in chartered accountancy, but some in certified and public finance accountancy. They have no preference for either degree subject or institution. This is proved by the fact that current students have come from traditional universities and the 'new' – for example John Moores, Oxford Brookes and Portsmouth.

They are looking for numerate all-rounders, with a strong academic record (minimum 2.2) and a high level of extra-curricular experience, achievement and experience.

Selection for interview is done by a paper sift of application forms. A checklist is used, taking account of:- GCSE maths and English passes, A-levels (although there is no points cut-off), expected degree class, evidence of initiative and level of responsibility, vacation and work experience, the quality of the additional personal information provided – plus accuracy, spelling and grammar.

☐ BUSINESS MANAGEMENT

BP are looking for outstanding graduates and post graduates to join BP as engineers, scientists or in commercial roles.

BP recruits people to work in all of BP's three core businesses. All our operations are conducted with clear commercial goals in mind. BP need people with the potential to becoming outstanding business managers. Marketers, traders and business analysts alike have to make assessments and decisions about the viability of deals as well as their financial potential, so graduates will need the capacity to understand quite complex production processes. A high standard of numeracy is essential this will be tested; language skills will be an additional asset.

Depending on which of the core businesses you choose, graduates will follow a structured and closely monitored training plan.

BP Chemicals commercial graduates will start off in an operational role in selling and sales support, commercial trading or logistics management. In BP Exploration graduates will join the Challenge Early Development Programme gaining a firm and essential understanding of the technical side of our operations while developing business skills.

In BP Oil you will undergo a full induction course and then follow the Merry-Go-Round scheme. This is a two year programme which allows you to do three real jobs: marketing or sales, business analysis and trading.

Interviews will be held at BP sites and some universities; as well as meeting professionals from your chosen discipline, graduates will be able to chat informally with recent BP graduates. In addition, graduates may be asked to complete a number of selection tests, questionnaires and group exercises.

In 1994 **Barclays** looked for 75 graduates for its nationally-run Management Development Programme and 40 for the Regional Management Training Programme, with a further three for marketing management. Any discipline is acceptable for all three programmes. Barclays is looking for team players with leadership potential and good communication skills.

They do not recruit from any favoured institutions but visit nearly all the universities that take part in the milk round – including those in Ulster and the Irish Republic.

Starting salary   MDP £16,150
                          RMTP £11,450

(1993 figures.)

Barclaycard expects its graduate entrants to become senior managers and has compiled a list of criteria applicants should meet initially; ability in:- decision making, planning and organising, understanding and presenting data; meeting a high standard of work, communication skill (in particular concise and accurate writing ability), persuasiveness, awareness of the effect of their behaviour on others and the ability to listen.

The company feels that a 2.1 in any subject demonstrates necessary intellectual ability and tests for the other qualities through verbal, numerical and personality tests and through group exercises at an assessment centre.

It accepts applicants from all universities but only occasionally from colleges of higher education.

Pilkington, the North West based glass manufacturer, recruits graduates with relevant degrees for technical work but considers applications from students in any subject for vacancies in sales and marketing and for places on its two year general management programme.

Applicants are assessed for organisational ability and reaction under pressure – through psychometric tests and through individual and team exercises.

Accountancy trainees must have a degree in a numerate discipline.

Eleven universities, with the exceptions of Birmingham and Cambridge, all in the north, are visited on the milk round. Candidates from other institutions apply direct.

Starting salary   £13,600

READING LIST

GENERAL

Cassell Careers Encyclopedia by Audrey Segal, Katherine Lea, published by Cassell Educational Ltd.

Getting into University and College published by Trotman.

CRAC Degree Course Guides published by Hobsons.

How to Choose Your Degree Course by Brian Heap, published by Trotman.

How to Complete Your UCAS Form by Stephen Lamley & Tony Higgins, published by Trotman.

The Natwest Student Book 1995 by Klaus Boehm & Jenny Lees-Spalding, published by Papermac.

The Complete Degree Course Offers for Entry into Higher Education by Brian Heap, published by Trotman.

Getting into Oxford and Cambridge published by Trotman.

The Potter Guide to Higher Education published by Dalebank Books.

Students' Money Matters published by Trotman.

Taking a Year Off by Val Butcher, published by Trotman.

The Times Good University Guide 1994-1995 by John O'Leary and Tom Cannon (Eds.), published by Times Books.

The UCAS Guide – 1995 entry published by UCAS.

University and College Entrance – The Official Guide published by UCAS.

The Time Out/NUS Student Guide published by Bloomsbury

Mature Students' Guide published by Trotman.

NatWest Students' Book published by MacMillan.

ACCOUNTANCY

AGCAS Guide to Accountancy, Taxation and Financial Management published by CSU (Publications) Ltd.

Becoming an Accountant by C. Nobes, published by Longmans.

Studying and the Examinations – The ACCA Syllabus published by ACCA.

Chartered Accountancy – The Essential Guide published by ICAEW.

A Finance Career at the Heart of Public Services – A Student's Guide to CIPFA published by CIPFA.

Understanding Company Financial Statements by P. H. Parker, published by Penguin.

An Illustrated Guide to Management Accounting published by CIMA.

A World of Opportunities – Careers in Finance published by ACCA.

BUSINESS

Corporate Strategy by Igor Ansoff, published by Penguin.

Employment Relations in Industrial Society by J. G. Goodman, published by Philip Allen.

AGCAS Guide to Management Services and Economic and Statistical Work published by CSU (Publications) Ltd.

Marketing Today by G. Oliver, published by Prentice Hall.

Psychology at Work by P. B. Warr, published by Penguin.

Quantitative Approaches in Business Studies by C. Morris, published by Pitman.

Small Business Guide by Colin Barrow, published by BBC Publications.

Small Businesses: Theirs ... or Yours – an AGCAS guide published by CSU (Publications) Ltd.

Trouble Shooter by John Harvey-Jones, published by BBC Publications.

Understanding Organisations by C. B. Handy, published by Penguin.

Economics

Blueprint for a Green Economy by David Pearce, Amil Markandya and Edward Barbier, published by Earthscan.

Understanding the British Economy by P. Donaldson.

Other references

Interview with Neil Clarke, Chairman of British Coal, by Rob Lewis in Business & Technology Journal published by Cromwell Media.

Higher Education in The Polytechnics and Colleges – Business & Management Studies published by DES/HMSO.

International Monetary Fund World Economic Outlook, October 1993 published by The I.M.F.

O.E.C.D. Economic Survey – The United Kingdom published by The O.E.C.D.

What is Quality in Higher Education by Diana Green (Ed.), published by SRHE and The Open University Press.

Professional and other non-academic bodies

The Chartered Association of Certified Accountants
29 Lincoln's Inn Fields
London
WC2A 3EE
Tel:071 242 6855

The Institute of Chartered Accountants in England and Wales
PO Box 433
Chartered Accountants' Hall
Moorgate Place
London
EC2P 2BJ
Tel:071 928 8100

The Institute of Chartered Accountants in Scotland
27 Queen Street
Edinburgh
EH2 1LA
Tel:031 225 5673

The Chartered Institute of Management Accountants
63 Portland Place
London
W1N 4AB
Tel:071 637 2311

The Chartered Institute of Public Finance and Accountancy
3 Robert Street
London
WC2N 6BH
Tel:071 895 8823 ext. 231

The Institute of Taxation
12 Upper Belgrave Street
London
SW1X 8BB
Tel:071 235 9381

The Institute of Administrative Management
40 Chatsworth Parade
Petts Wood
Orpington
BR5 1RW

The Association of British Chambers of Commerce
9 Tufton Street
London
SW1P 3GB
Tel:071 222 1555

The Institute of Chartered Secretaries and Administrators
16 Park Crescent
London
W1N 4AH
Tel:071 580 4741

The Institute of Credit Management
The Water Mill
Station Road
South Luffenham
Oakham
Leicestershire
LE15 8NB
Tel:0780 721888

The Institute of Data Processing Management
IDPM House
Edgington Way
Ruxley Corner
Sidcup
Kent
DA14 5HR

The Confederation of British Industry
Centrepoint
103 New Oxford Street
London
WC1A 1DU
Tel:071 379 7400

Graduate Enterprise Programme
Mr Ian Robinson E540
Training Enterprise and Education Directorate
Moorfood
Sheffield
S1 4PQ

The Industrial Society
3 Carlton House Terrace
London
SW1Y 5DG
Tel:071 839 4300

The Institute of Information Scientists
44 Museum Street
London
WC1A 1LY
Tel:071 831 8003

Institute of Management Consultants
5th Floor
32/33 Hatton Garden
London
EC1N 8DL
Tel:071 242 2140

Management Consultancies Organisation
11 Wst Halkin Street
London
SW1X 8JL
Tel:071 235 3897

The Institute of Management Services
1 Cecil Court
London Road
Enfield
Middlesex
EN2 6DD

The Chartered Institute of Marketing
Moor Hall
Cookham
Berks
SL6 9QH
Tel:0628 524922

The Operational Research Society
Neville House
Waterloo Street
Birmingham
B2 5TX

The Institute of Packaging
Sysonby Lodge
Nottingham Road
Melton Mowbray
Leicestershire
LE13 0NU
Tel:0664 500055

The Institute of Personnel Management
IPM House
Camp Road
Wimbledon
London
SW19 4UX
Tel:081 946 9100

The Prince's Youth Business Trust
5 Cleveland Place
London
SW1Y 6JJ
Tel:071 321 6500

The Chartered Institute of Purchasing and Supply
Easton House
Easton on the Hill
Stamford
Lincolnshire
PE9 3NZ
Tel:0780 56777

The Institute of Sales and Marketing Managemen
31 Upper George Street
Luton
Bedfordshire
LU1 2RD

The Federation of Small Businesses
32 St Annes Road West
Lytham St Annes
Lancs
FY8 1NY
Tel:0253 720911

THE TABLES

This section is sub-divided to make it easier to use. The sections are:

The questionnaire; a worked example; questionnaire results; the tables

☐ THE QUESTIONNAIRE

QUESTIONNAIRE OF YOUR PREFERENCES

1)	WHICH AREA(S) WOULD YOU LIKE TO STUDY IN?				
		Yes	?	No	Refer to the first part of chapter four to help you make your decision – remember the main points to consider. You can look at column one of the tables to see which areas the various universities are in. Remember that you are deciding where you want to spend the best three years of your life!
1	London				
2	South-East England				
3	South-West England				
4	The Midlands				
5	Eastern England				
6	North-East England				
7	North-West England				
8	Northern Ireland				
9	Wales				
10	Scotland				

2)	**WHAT TYPE AND STRUCTURE OF UNIVERSITY WOULD YOU LIKE TO ATTEND ?**					
		Yes	?	No	Symbol	
	Old Uni – campus				●◆	
	Old Uni – multisite				●❖	
	New Uni – campus				☐◆	
	New Uni – multisite				☐❖	
	Poly – multisite				✠❖	
	College etc. – campus				✠◆	
	College etc. – multisite				✠❖	

3)	**WHAT TYPE OF COURSE WOULD YOU LIKE TO DO ?**			
		Yes	?	No
	Single Hons			
	Combined/Joint Hons			
	With a language			
	As a sandwich course			
	With study abroad			

4)	**WHAT ARE YOUR SUBJECT CHOICES ?**			
		Single Hons?	Combined?	Joint?
	1)			
	2)			
	3)			
	4)			
	5)			
	6)			
	7)			
	8)			
	9)			

5)	WHAT QUALIFICATION WOULD YOU LIKE TO STUDY FOR ?				
		Yes	?	No	
	Degree				
	HND				
	Other				
6)	**WHAT IS YOUR PREFERRED LENGTH OF COURSE ?**				
		Yes	?	No	
	1 Year				
	2 Years				
	3 Years				
	4 Years				
	5 Years				
7)	**WHAT GRADES DO YOU EXPECT TO GET AT A-LEVEL ?**				
	Subject	Level		Grade	Points

☐ A WORKED EXAMPLE

Here's an example of how to work down through the tables once you have completed the questionnaire.

We'll suppose that, after some thought, you've decided that you want to study an Economics-based degree and that:

1. There are four areas you're interested in – London, South-East England, South-West England and The Midlands.

Step 1: Highlight your area Go through the Economics table highlighting institutions in areas 1, 2, 3 and 4 – London, South-East England, South-West England and The Midlands. If you really wouldn't consider any other areas then cross out all institutions in those areas.

2. You want to study Economics and French.

Step 2: Highlight your course Go through the table again highlighting Economics and French courses at the institutions you picked out in Step 1.

3. You'd prefer to go to an Old University but you'd consider trying to get on to courses run at New Universities and colleges in those areas. You don't mind whether you end up in a single- or multi-site campus.

Step 3: Choose the type of institution you want to study at
Since in this case you are not sure you want only the Old Universities and you don't mind what type of campus you end up on you do not have to highlight any institutions or cross any out. Make a note of them all.

4. You're hoping to get 2 Bs and a C in your A-Levels.

Step 4: Find out where you could study – check the grades
Then look at the grades and highlight all the courses where:
a) the requirements are BBC and under or,
b) 22 points and less or,
c) they don't specify requirements.

Step 5: Make your shortlist Below is a Shortlist of courses which matches your requirements – there's a blank one in Section 3 for you to fill in when you do this exercise for yourself.

University	Type	Course	Requirements
Buckingham	OLD	ECON WITH FR	12
East Anglia	OLD	ECON WITH LANG	BBC
East London	NEW	FR/ECON	-
Kent	OLD	EUR ECON/FR	BCC
Lon, QM &WC	OLD	FR & ECON	BCC
Royal Holloway	COLL.	ECON WITH FR	BCC
Middlesex	NEW	EUR ECON – FR	8-12
Oxford Brookes	NEW	E/FR,FR LANG CONT ST	-
Plymouth	OLD	ECON (APPL) WITH LANG	L
Reading	OLD	FR & ECON	BBC
Southampton	OLD	ECON & FR	22
Surrey	OLD	FR/ECON WITH INTL BUS	BBC
Sussex	OLD	ECON WITH FR(MAITRISE)	BCC
Thames Valley	NEW	ECON WTH FR	8

A shortlist of courses – the worked example (Section 1)

You can find the addresses and phone numbers for all the courses in the tables at the back of the book if you want to use your shortlist as a mailing list for your prospectus requests. Alternatively, you can enter the courses directly into the prioritisation grid in Section 4.

☐ QUESTIONNAIRE RESULTS

QUESTIONNAIRE RESULTS – SHORTLIST OF COURSES

	WHAT ARE YOUR SUBJECT CHOICES ?			
	University	Type	Course	Requirements
1)				
2)				
3)				
4)				
5)				
6)				
7)				
8)				
9)				
10)				
11)				
12)				
13)				
14)				
15)				
16)				
17)				
18)				

This is your shortlist – your mailing list for prospectuses. You should copy the courses on to the preference grid in Section 4. When you've got all the information you need you can use the preference grid to rank the courses and to find out which ones you're going to put onto your UCAS form.

☐ KEY TO TERMS AND SYMBOLS USED IN THE TABLES AND TEXT:

●	Old Universities
☐	Ex-Polytechnics now Universities
◆	Campus universities
❖	Multi-site or multi-campus university or college
✠	College
‡ OR *	Refer to the prospectus
▼	Refer to the institution
+ OR £	Maths or Economics (as requirements for the course)
COLL	College
COMB	Combined / Joint courses
DEG	Degree
DIP	Diploma
HE	Higher Education
HND	Higher National Diploma
L	Language (as requirements for the course)
MOD	Module
OPT	Options
POLY	Polytechnic
S	Single Honours
SC	Science
ST	Studies
Multigps	Multi-disciplinary Groups
J/D HONS	Joint or Double Hons
e.g. 18	No. of points

TABLE A – ACCOUNTANCY COURSES

COLLEGE DETAILS					COURSE DETAILS						ENTRY		
REGION	NAME	TYPE	VALUE ADDED	EMPLOYMENT	SUBJECT	TYPE	DURATION	SANDWICH	SUBJECTS REQ	GRADES REQ	APPLY	GET ON	% GET ON
1	CITY UNIVERSITY	●◆	4	41	ECONOMICS/ACCOUNTANCY	S	3			BCC			
1	EAST LONDON UNIVERSITY	□◆	45	95	ACCOUNTING & FINANCE	S	3	‡		DDD-CD	563	45	8
1	GREENWICH UNIVERSITY	□◆	79	84	ACCOUNTANCY & FINANCE	S	3		‡	12	718	161	22
1	GUILDHALL UNIVERSITY	□◆	55	79	ACCOUNTING	S	3			CCC	872	68	8
1	KINGSTON UNIVERSITY	□◆	69	28	ACCOUNTING & FINANCE	S	3			CCD	847	91	11
1	KINGSTON UNIVERSITY	□◆	69	28	ACCOUNTING & LAW	S	3			CCC			
1	LONDON SCHOOL OF ECONOMICS	●◆	22	90	ACCOUNTING & FINANCE	S	3			24	885	30	3
1	MIDDLESEX UNIVERSITY	□◆	91	3	ACCOUNTING & FINANCE	S	3			14			
1	NORTH LONDON UNIVERSITY	□◆	35	55	ACCOUNTING & FINANCE	S	3			16			
1	SOUTH BANK UNIVERSITY	□◆	69	19	ACCOUNTING & FINANCE	S	3			CCD	914	102	11
1	SOUTH BANK UNIVERSITY	□◆	69	19	BUSINESS ACCOUNTING	S	3	‡		▶	NEW		
1	SOUTH BANK UNIVERSITY	□◆	69	19	FOUNDATION ACCOUNTING	S	3*	‡		12			
1	THAMES VALLEY UNIVERSITY	□◆	63	24	ACCOUNTING STUDIES EUROPE	S	3		L	14			
1	THAMES VALLEY UNIVERSITY	□◆	63	24	ACCOUNTING & FINANCE	S	3			12	269	57	21
1	THAMES VALLEY UNIVERSITY	□◆	63	24	ACCOUNTING & LAW	S	3			16			
2	BOURNEMOUTH UNIVERSITY	□◆	55	34	ACCOUNTING	S	3	▶		16			
2	BRIGHTON UNIVERSITY	□◆	47	12	ACCOUNTING & FINANCE	S	3	4	‡	16	823	85	10
2	BRIGHTON UNIVERSITY	□◆	47	12	ACCOUNTING & LAW	S	3	4	‡	18	NEW		
2	BRIGHTON UNIVERSITY	□◆	47	12	INTERNATIONAL ACCOUNTING & FINANCE	S	3	4	‡	18			
2	KENT UNIVERSITY	●◆	47	74	ACCOUNTING	S	3			20	543	35	6
2	KENT UNIVERSITY	●◆	47	74	ACCOUNTING WITH COMPUTING	S	3			20	139	9	6

	University				Course							
2	KENT UNIVERSITY	●◆	47	74	ACCOUNTING/ECONOMICS	J	3			20		
2	KENT UNIVERSITY	●◆	47	74	ACCOUNTING/SOC POL & ADMIN	J	3			20		
2	KENT UNIVERSITY	●◆	47	74	IR (ACCOUNTING)	S	3			20		
2	KENT UNIVERSITY	●◆	47	74	MATHEMATICS & ACCOUNTING	S	3/4	+		20		
2	PORTSMOUTH UNIVERSITY	□◆	61	14	ACCOUNTING	S	3	4	14	521	81	16
2	PORTSMOUTH UNIVERSITY	□◆	61	14	ACCOUNTING & BUSINESS INFO SYSTEMS	S	3	4	12	NEW		
2	PORTSMOUTH UNIVERSITY	□◆	61	14	ACCOUNTING & ECONOMICS	S	3	4	14	NEW		
2	READING UNIVERSITY	●◆	85	55	ACCOUNTING & ECONOMICS	S	3		BBC			
2	SOUTHAMPTON INSTITUTE	✳◆	N/A	N/A	ACCOUNTANCY	S	3		10	318	102	32
2	SOUTHAMPTON INSTITUTE	✳◆	N/A	N/A	ACCOUNTANCY & LAW	S	3		10			
2	SOUTHAMPTON UNIVERSITY	●◆	35	74	ACCOUNTING & ECONOMICS	J	3		22			
2	SOUTHAMPTON UNIVERSITY	●◆	35	74	ACCOUNTING & FINANCE	J	3		22			
2	SOUTHAMPTON UNIVERSITY	●◆	35	74	ACCOUNTING & FRENCH, GER, SPAN, PORT	J	4		22			
2	SOUTHAMPTON UNIVERSITY	●◆	35	74	ACCOUNTING & LAW	J	3		22			
2	SOUTHAMPTON UNIVERSITY	●◆	35	74	ACCOUNTING & STATISTICS	J	3		22			
2	SOUTHAMPTON UNIVERSITY	●◆	35	74	BUSINESS ECONOMICS & ACCOUNTING	J	3		22			
3	BRISTOL UNIVERSITY	●◆	14	67	ECON & ACC WITH STUDY IN CONT. EUROPE	S	4	+ & L	ABC-BBC	NEW		
3	BRISTOL UNIVERSITY	●◆	14	67	ECONOMICS & ACCOUNTING	S	3	+ & L	ABC-BBC			
3	BRISTOL UNIVERSITY (UWE)	●◆	35	30	ACCOUNTING & FINANCE	S	3	4	CCC-BB	969	104	11
3	EXETER UNIVERSITY	●◆	1	62	ACCOUNTANCY STUDIES	S	3		BBB	464	39	8
3	EXETER UNIVERSITY	●◆	1	62	ACCOUNTANCY WITH EUROPEAN STUDY	S	4	L	BBB	28	1	4
3	PLYMOUTH UNIVERSITY	□◆	55	34	ACCOUNTING & FINANCE	S	3		CCD			
3	PLYMOUTH UNIVERSITY	□◆	55	34	ECONOMICS (APPLIED) WITH ACCOUNTING	S	3	‡	▶			
3	PLYMOUTH UNIVERSITY	□◆	55	34	LAW WITH ACCOUNTING	S	3	‡	▶			
4	BIRMINGHAM UNIVERSITY	●◆	85	67	BCom (ACCOUNTING) HONS	S	3		BBC	632	59	9
4	BIRMINGHAM UNIVERSITY	●◆	85	67	BCom (ACCOUNTING) WITH FRENCH	S	4	‡	BBC	47	5	11
4	BUCKINGHAM UNIVERSITY	●◆	46	1	ACCOUNTING WITH ECONOMICS	S	2		18	17		
4	BUCKINGHAM UNIVERSITY	●◆	46	1	ACCOUNTING WITH INSURANCE	S	2		18	5		

TABLE A - ACCOUNTANCY COURSES (Continued)

REGION	NAME	TYPE	VALUE ADDED	EMPLOYMENT	SUBJECT	TYPE	DURATION	SANDWICH	SUBJECTS REQ	GRADES REQ	APPLY	GET ON	%
4	BUCKINGHAM UNIVERSITY	●◆	46	1	ACCOUNTING & FINANCIAL MANAGEMENT	S	2			18	204	7	3
4	BUCKINGHAM UNIVERSITY	●◆	46	1	COMPUTER SCIENCE WITH ACCOUNTING	S	2			12	17	4	24
4	CENTRAL ENGLAND UNIVERSITY	□◆	53	14	ACCOUNTANCY	S	3			18-16	1076	86	8
4	COVENTRY UNIVERSITY	□◆	47	18	ACCOUNTING	S	3		‡	14			
4	DERBY UNIVERSITY	□◆	69	90	ACCOUNTING	S	3			12	NEW		
4	LOUGHBOROUGH UNIVERSITY	●◆	41	34	ACCOUNTING & FINANCIAL MANAGEMENT	S	3	4		BBC	576	47	8
4	LOUGHBOROUGH UNIVERSITY	●◆	41	34	ECONOMICS WITH ACCOUNTANCY	S	3		‡	BBC	233	23	10
4	LUTON COLLEGE OF H.E.	✱◆	N/A	N/A	ACCOUNTING	S	3	+		12	155	75	48
4	NENE COLLEGE	✱◆	N/A	N/A	ACCOUNTANCY & FINANCE	S	3	+		▶			
4	NOTTINGHAM TRENT UNIVERSITY	□◆	31	14	ACCOUNTING & FINANCE	S	3	4	‡	CCE	1896	59	3
4	NOTTINGHAM UNIVERSITY	●◆	88	28	INDUSTRIAL ECONOMICS WITH ACCOUNTING	S	3			BBB			
4	OXFORD BROOKES UNIVERSITY	□◆	31	12	ACCOUNTING (& 11 MOD OPT) 3	J	3/4						
4	OXFORD BROOKES UNIVERSITY	□◆	31	12	(31 MOD OPT &) ACCOUNTING 3	J	3						
4	STAFFORDSHIRE UNIVERSITY	□◆	63	47	ACCOUNTING & COMPUTING	S	3			CC			
4	STAFFORDSHIRE UNIVERSITY	□◆	63	47	ACCOUNTING & LAW	S	3			BC-BCC			
4	STAFFORDSHIRE UNIVERSITY	□◆	63	47	INFORMATION SYSTEMS & ACCOUNTING	S	3			BC-BCC			
4	WARWICK UNIVERSITY	●◆	19	55	ACCOUNTING & FINANCIAL ANALYSIS	S	3			BBB	575	40	7
4	WOLVERHAMPTON UNIVERSITY	●◆	91	50	ACCOUNTING & FINANCE	S	3	4		16			
5	EAST ANGLIA UNIVERSITY	●◆	13	79	ACCOUNTANCY	S	3		‡	BBC	432	55	13
5	EAST ANGLIA UNIVERSITY	◆	13	79	ACCOUNTANCY WITH A EUROPEAN LANGUAGE	S	3		‡	BBB-BBC			
5	EAST ANGLIA UNIVERSITY	●◆	13	79	ACCOUNTANCY WITH LAW	S	3		‡	BBC-BBD			

				University	Course				Grades			
5	●◆	10	79	ESSEX UNIVERSITY	ACCOUNTING & FINANCIAL MANAGEMENT	S	3		BBC	685	54	8
6	●◆	10	79	ESSEX UNIVERSITY	ACCOUNTING, FINANCE & ECONOMICS	J	3	+	BCC			
5	●◆	10	79	ESSEX UNIVERSITY	INFO. MANAGEMENT WITH ACCOUNTING	S	3	+	20	156	21	13
5	□◆	79	3	HERTFORDSHIRE UNIVERSITY	ACCOUNTING & MGT INFO SYSTEMS	S	3	‡	16			
5	●●	47	62	HULL UNIVERSITY	BSc ACCOUNTING	S	3	‡	BCC	464	51	11
5	●●	47	62	HULL UNIVERSITY	ECONOMICS & ACCOUNTING	S	3	‡	BBC			
5	□◆	79	55	HUMBERSIDE UNIVERSITY	ACCOUNTANCY & FINANCE	S	3		16	412	35	8
5	✱	N/A	N/A	SUFFOLK COLLEGE	BUSINESS STUDIES WITH ACCOUNTING	S	3		▶			
6	□◆	63	41	HUDDERSFIELD UNIVERSITY	ACCOUNTANCY STUDIES	S	3		CC	481	128	27
6	□◆	91	8	LEEDS METRO UNIVERSITY	ACCOUNTING & FINANCE	S	3	4	CC Approx	1806	49	3
6	□◆	91	8	LEEDS METRO UNIVERSITY	EUROPEAN FINANCE & ACCOUNTING	S	3	‡	CCD-CC	271	68	25
6	●◆	41	62	LEEDS UNIVERSITY	ACCOUNTING & FINANCE	S	3		BBB	1335	38	3
6	●●	41	62	LEEDS UNIVERSITY	ACCOUNTING-COMPUTER SCIENCE	J	3/4	+	BBC			
6	●●	41	62	LEEDS UNIVERSITY	ACCOUNTING-INFORMATION SYSTEMS	J	3/4		BBC			
6	●●	41	62	LEEDS UNIVERSITY	ACCOUNTING-OPERATIONAL RESEARCH	J	3/4	+	BBC			
6	●●	19	34	NEWCASTLE UNIVERSITY	ACCOUNTING & COMPUTER SCIENCE	J	3	+	BCC			
6	●●	19	34	NEWCASTLE UNIVERSITY	ACCOUNTING & FINANCIAL ANALYSIS	S	3		BBC	489	36	7
6	●●	19	34	NEWCASTLE UNIVERSITY	ACCOUNTING & LAW	S	3		BBB			
6	●●	19	34	NEWCASTLE UNIVERSITY	ACCOUNTING & MATHS	J	3	+	BCC			
6	●●	19	34	NEWCASTLE UNIVERSITY	ACCOUNTING & STATISTICS	J	3	+	BCC			
6	●●	19	34	NEWCASTLE UNIVERSITY	ECONOMICS & ACCOUNTING	S	3		BBC			
6	●●	19	34	NEWCASTLE UNIVERSITY	FRENCH WITH ACCOUNTING	S	4		BBB	498	20	4
6	●●	19	34	NEWCASTLE UNIVERSITY	GERMAN WITH ACCOUNTING	S	4		20	158	11	7
6	●●	19	34	NEWCASTLE UNIVERSITY	SPANISH WITH ACCOUNTING	S	4		BBB	183	16	9
6	□◆	47	88	NORTHUMBRIA UNIVERSITY	ACCOUNTANCY	S	3	‡	16	728	85	12
6	□◆	47	88	NORTHUMBRIA UNIVERSITY	ACCOUNTANCY & FINANCE - HND	S	2	‡	8	295	22	7
6	□◆	47	88	NORTHUMBRIA UNIVERSITY	ACCOUNTING - diploma	S	2	‡	8	NEW		
6	□◆	63	50	SHEFFIELD HALLAM UNIVERSITY	ACCOUNTING & COMBINED STUDIES	J						

TABLE A – ACCOUNTANCY COURSES (Continued)

REGION	COLLEGE DETAILS				COURSE DETAILS						ENTRY		
	NAME	TYPE	VALUE ADDED	EMPLOYMENT	SUBJECT	TYPE	DURATION	SANDWICH	SUBJECTS REQ	GRADES REQ	APPLY		% GET ON
6	SHEFFIELD HALLAM UNIVERSITY	□◆	63	50	ACCOUNTING & MANAGEMENT CONTROL	S	3	4	‡	14	1105	81	7
6	SHEFFIELD UNIVERSITY	◆◆	10	47	ACC & FINANCIAL MGT/COMPUTER SCIENCE	S	3		+	BBC			
6	SHEFFIELD UNIVERSITY	◆◆	10	47	ACC & FINANCIAL MGT/INFORMATION MGT	S	3			BBB			
6	SHEFFIELD UNIVERSITY	◆◆	10	47	ACCOUNTING & FIN MGT/MATHS	S	3		+	BBC			
6	SHEFFIELD UNIVERSITY	◆◆	10	47	ACCOUNTING & FINANCE MGT	S	3			BBB	935	40	
6	SHEFFIELD UNIVERSITY	◆◆	10	47	ACCOUNTING & FINANCIAL MGT/ECONOMICS	S	3		‡	BBB			
6	SUNDERLAND UNIVERSITY	◆◆	75	94	ACCOUNTING & BUSINESS	S	3		‡	14	266	53	
6	SUNDERLAND UNIVERSITY	◆◆	75	94	ACCOUNTING & COMPUTING	S	3	4	+	CCC			4
6	SUNDERLAND UNIVERSITY	◆◆	75	94	ACCOUNTING & MATHS	S	3		+	CCC			
6	TEESSIDE UNIVERSITY	◆◆	75	79	ACCOUNTING & FINANCE	S	3/4		‡	CCD			
6	TEESSIDE UNIVERSITY	◆◆	75	79	ACCOUNTING & LAW	S	3		‡	CCD			
7	BOLTON INSTITUTE	‡◆◆	N/A	N/A	ACCOUNTANCY (& 20 COMB OPT) 1	J	3			14-10			
7	CENTRAL LANCS UNIVERSITY	◆◆	41	92	ACCOUNTING	S	3			16			
7	LANCASTER UNIVERSITY	◆◆	62	62	ACCOUNTING & FINANCE	S	3		‡	22	750	113	15
7	LANCASTER UNIVERSITY	◆◆	62	62	ACCOUNTING-ECONOMICS	S	3		‡	22	722	39	5
7	LANCASTER UNIVERSITY	◆◆	62	62	ACCOUNTING,FINANCE - COMPUTER STUDIES	S	3		+	22			
7	LANCASTER UNIVERSITY	◆◆	62	62	ACCOUNTING,FINANCE - MATHS	S	3		+	22			
7	L'POOL JOHN MOORES UNIVERSITY	□◆	69	30	ACCOUNTING & FINANCE	S	3		‡	16-14	1143	53	5
7	LIVERPOOL UNIVERSITY	◆◆	22	78	ACCOUNTING	S	3		‡	CCC	638	22	3
7	LIVERPOOL UNIVERSITY	◆◆	22	78	ACCOUNTING & COMPUTER SCIENCE	J	3		‡	CCC			
7	LIVERPOOL UNIVERSITY	◆◆	22	78	MANAGEMENT ECONOMICS & ACCOUNTING	J	3		‡	BCC			

	Institution				Course				Grade			
7	MANCHESTER UNIVERSITY	◆◆	7	67	ACCOUNTING & LAW	J	4	‡	BBB			
7	MANCHESTER UNIVERSITY	◆◆	7	67	COMPUTER SCIENCE & ACCOUNTING	S	3	‡	BCC			
7	SALFORD UNIVERSITY	◆◆	88	19	FINANCE & ACCOUNTING	S	3		BBC	433	68	16
8	QUEEN'S UNIVERSITY, BELFAST	◆◆	18	55	ACCOUNTING	S	3		ABB	403	43	11
8	QUEEN'S UNIVERSITY, BELFAST	◆◆	18	55	ACCOUNTING WITH FRENCH	S	3		ABB	47	4	9
8	QUEEN'S UNIVERSITY, BELFAST	◆◆	18	55	ACCOUNTING WITH SPANISH	S	3		ABB			
8	QUEEN'S UNIVERSITY, BELFAST	◆◆	18	55	LAW & ACCOUNTING	S	4		ABB			
8	ULSTER UNIVERSITY	◆◆	69	30	ACCOUNTING (Specialisms)	S	3		BBB-BBC	697	76	11
8	ULSTER UNIVERSITY	◆◆	69	30	ACCOUNTING(DipHE)	S			DD			
9	CARDIFF UNIVERSITY	◆◆◆	19	74	ACCOUNTING	S	3		BBC	324	58	18
9	CARDIFF UNIVERSITY	◆◆	19	74	ACCOUNTING WITH FRENCH, GER, ITAL, SPAN	S	4	L	BBC	NEW		
9	CARDIFF UNIVERSITY	◆◆	19	74	ACCOUNTING & ECONOMICS	S	3		BBC			
9	CARDIFF UNIVERSITY	◆◆	19	74	ACCOUNTING & MANAGEMENT	S	4		BBC			
9	GLAMORGAN UNIVERSITY	◆◆	55	95	ACCOUNTING & FINANCE	S	3	4 ‡	14	358	63	18
9	GLAMORGAN UNIVERSITY	◆◆	55	95	COMPUTING & ACCOUNTING	S	3	4 ‡	10	NEW		
9	GWENT COLLEGE	◆◆◆	N/A	N/A	ACCOUNTING & FINANCE	S	3	‡	10			
9	GWENT COLLEGE	◆◆◆	N/A	N/A	ACCOUNTING & FINANCE - HND	S	2	‡	10			
9	GWENT COLLEGE	◆◆◆	N/A	N/A	ACCOUNTING & LEGAL STUDIES	S	3	‡	10			
9	GWENT COLLEGE	◆◆	N/A	N/A	BUSINESS & ACCOUNTING	S	3	‡	10			
9	SWANSEA INSTITUTE	◆◆◆	N/A	N/A	ACCOUNTING	S	3	‡	10	80	18	23
9	UNIV COLL OF N. WALES,BANGOR	◆◆	15	88	ACCOUNTING & FINANCE	S	3		BCC	382	22	6
9	UNIV COLL OF N. WALES,BANGOR	◆◆	15	88	ACCOUNTING/BANKING	J	3		BCC	30		
9	UNIV COLL OF N. WALES,BANGOR	◆◆	15	88	ACCOUNTING/ECONOMICS	J	3		BCC			
9	UNIV COLL OF N. WALES,BANGOR	◆◆	15	88	ACCOUNTING/FRENCH (SYLL A)	J	4		BCC			
9	UNIV COLL OF N. WALES,BANGOR	◆◆	15	88	ACCOUNTING/FRENCH (SYLL B)	J	4		BCC			
9	UNIV COLL OF N. WALES,BANGOR	◆◆◆	15	88	ACCOUNTING/GERMAN,RUSSIAN	J	4		BCC			
9	UNIV COLL OF N. WALES,BANGOR	◆◆	15	88	ACCOUNTING/MATHS	J	3		18			
9	UNIV COLL OF N. WALES,BANGOR	◆◆	15	88	ACCOUNTING/MODERN LANGUAGE	J	4		18			

TABLE A - ACCOUNTANCY COURSES (Continued)

| | COLLEGE DETAILS | | | | COURSE DETAILS | | | | | | ENTRY | | |
REGION	NAME	TYPE	VALUE ADDED	EMPLOYMENT	SUBJECT	TYPE	DURATION	SANDWICH	SUBJECTS REQ	GRADES REQ	APPLY	GET ON	%
9	UNIV OF WALES, ABERYSTWYTH	❖❖	47	41	ACCOUNTING & FINANCE	S	3			BCC	207	32	15
9	UNIV OF WALES, ABERYSTWYTH	❖❖	47	41	ACCOUNTING & FINANCE WITH EURO LANG	S	4			BCC	28		
9	UNIV OF WALES, ABERYSTWYTH	❖❖	47	41	ACCOUNTING & FINANCE WITH WELSH	S	3			BCC			
9	UNIV OF WALES, ABERYSTWYTH	❖❖	47	41	ACCOUNTING & FINANCE & ECONOMICS	S	3			BCC			
9	UNIV OF WALES, ABERYSTWYTH	❖❖	47	41	ACCOUNTING & FINANCE & LAW	S	3			BBB-BBC			
9	UNIV OF WALES, ABERYSTWYTH	❖❖	47	41	ACCOUNTING (& 7 COMB OPT) 4	J	3						
9	UNIV OF WALES, ABERYSTWYTH	❖❖	47	41	INFO MGT. ACCOUNTING & FINANCE	J	3			20			
10	ABERDEEN UNIVERSITY	❖❖	47	41	ACCOUNTANCY	S	3/4	‡		BBC	5070	757	15
10	ABERDEEN UNIVERSITY	❖❖	47	41	ACCOUNTANCY (& 10 OPT) 2	J	4/5	‡		BBC	5070	757	15
10	ABERDEEN UNIVERSITY	❖❖	47	41	PHILOSOPHY WITH ACCOUNTING	S	4	‡		BBC			
10	DUNDEE INSTITUTE	❖❖	N/A	N/A	ACCOUNTING	S	3 4	‡		12	72		
10	DUNDEE INSTITUTE	❖❖	N/A	N/A	ACCOUNTING - HND	S	2	‡		12	44		
10	DUNDEE UNIVERSITY	❖❖	9	30	ACCOUNTANCY - BAcc	S	4	‡		BCC	552	96	17
10	DUNDEE UNIVERSITY	❖❖	9	30	ACCOUNTANCY & CHEMISTRY	S	4	‡		BC-CDD	2516	223	9
10	DUNDEE UNIVERSITY	❖❖	9	30	ACCOUNTANCY & COMPUTER SCIENCE	B	4	‡		BC-CDD	2516	223	9
10	DUNDEE UNIVERSITY	❖❖	9	30	ACCOUNTANCY & MATHEMATICS	S	4	‡		BC-CDD	2516	223	9
10	EDINBURGH UNIVERSITY	❖❖	26	50	BUSINESS STUDIES & ACCOUNTING	J	4	‡		BBC			
10	EDINBURGH UNIVERSITY	❖❖	26	50	ECONOMICS & ACCOUNTING	S	4			BBC			
10	EDINBURGH UNIVERSITY	❖❖	26	50	LAW & ACCOUNTANCY	S	4			ABB			
10	GLASGOW CAL UNIVERSITY	❖❖	63	47	ACCOUNTANCY	S	3 4	+		BB	863	108	13
10	GLASGOW CAL UNIVERSITY	❖❖	63	47	ACCOUNTANCY - HND	S	2	+		CC	33	1	3

	University	Course		Code1	Code2		Yr		Grade	N1	N2	N3
10	HERIOT-WATT UNIVERSITY	ACCOUNTANCY WITH FRENCH	●●	22	50	S	4	‡	BBC	10		
10	HERIOT-WATT UNIVERSITY	ACCOUNTANCY WITH GERMAN	●●	22	50	S	4	‡	BBC	2		
10	HERIOT-WATT UNIVERSITY	ACCOUNTANCY WITH SPANISH	●◆	22	50	S	4	‡	BBC			
10	HERIOT-WATT UNIVERSITY	ACCOUNTANCY & FINANCE	●◆	22	50	S	3 4	+	BBC	387	42	11
10	HERIOT-WATT UNIVERSITY	ACCOUNTANCY & INFORMATION MGT.	●●	22	50	S	4	+	BBC			
10	NAPIER UNIVERSITY	ACCOUNTING	□◆	55	19	S	3	‡	CCC			
10	NAPIER UNIVERSITY	ACCOUNTING - HND	□◆	55	19	S	2	‡	CC			
10	PAISLEY UNIVERSITY	ACCOUNTING	□◆	26	55	S	3	4	CCC			
10	ROBERT GORDON UNIVERSITY	ACCOUNTING & FINANCE	□◆	87	3	S	3	4	BCC			
10	STIRLING UNIVERSITY	ACCOUNTANCY	●◆	31	41	S	4	‡	BBC	496	46	9
10	STIRLING UNIVERSITY	ACCOUNTANCY/BUSINESS STUDIES	●◆	31	41	S	4		BBC			
10	STIRLING UNIVERSITY	ACCOUNTANCY/COMPUTER SCIENCE	●◆	31	41	S	4		BBC			
10	STIRLING UNIVERSITY	ACCOUNTANCY/ECONOMICS	●◆	31	41	S	4		BBC			
10	STIRLING UNIVERSITY	ACCOUNTANCY/FRENCH, GER, SPAN LANGUAGE	●◆	31	41	S	4	‡	BBC			
10	STIRLING UNIVERSITY	ACCOUNTANCY/MANAGEMENT SCIENCE	●◆	31	41	S	4		BBC			
10	STIRLING UNIVERSITY	ACCOUNTANCY/MARKETING	●◆	31	41	S	4		BBC			
10	STIRLING UNIVERSITY	ACCOUNTANCY/MATHS	●◆	31	41	S	4	‡	BBC			
10	STRATHCLYDE UNIVERSITY	ACCOUNTING	●◆	88	41	S	3/4	+	BBC	519	58	11
10	STRATHCLYDE UNIVERSITY	MATHS, STATISTICS & ACCOUNTING	●◆	88	41	S	3/4	+	BBC			

TABLE B – BUSINESS STUDIES COURSES

	COLLEGE DETAILS				COURSE DETAILS						ENTRY		
REGION	NAME	TYPE	VALUE ADDED	EMPLOYMENT	SUBJECT	TYPE	DURATION	SANDWICH	SUBJECTS REQ	GRADES REQ	APPLY	GET ON	%
1	CITY UNIVERSITY	●◆	4	41	BUSINESS STUDIES WITH LANGUAGE	S							
1	CITY UNIVERSITY	●◆	4	41	BUSINESS STUDIES WITH LANGUAGE OPTION	S	3 4	‡		24	1346	73	5
1	EAST LONDON UNIVERSITY	□◆	45	95	BUSINESS STUDIES WITH SPECIALISMS	S	4	‡					
1	EAST LONDON UNIVERSITY	□◆	45	95	BUSINESS STUDIES & (36 COMB OPT) 16	J	3/4	‡					
1	EAST LONDON UNIVERSITY	□◆	45	95	BUSINESS AND FINANCE - HND	S	2	‡			488	58	12
1	GREENWICH UNIVERSITY	□◆	79	84	BUSINESS & MEDIA COMMUNICATIONS	S	3	‡		12	NEW		
1	GREENWICH UNIVERSITY	□◆	79	84	BUSINESS ADMINISTRATION	S	3			12	100	91	91
1	GREENWICH UNIVERSITY	□◆	79	84	BUSINESS AND RETAIL SERVICE	S	3	‡		12	NEW		
1	GREENWICH UNIVERSITY	□◆	79	84	BUSINESS AND FINANCE (OPTIONS) - HND	S	2	‡		6 Approx	611	178	29
1	GREENWICH UNIVERSITY	□◆	79	84	BUSINESS STUDIES	S	2	‡		CCD-BC			
1	GREENWICH UNIVERSITY	□◆	79	84	INTERNATIONAL BUSINESS (NEW EUROPE)	S	3 4	‡		16	NEW		
1	GREENWICH UNIVERSITY	□◆	79	84	BUSINESS AND FINANCE (TRAV & TOUR) - HND	S	2	‡		6 Approx	NEW		
1	GUILDHALL UNIVERSITY	□◆	55	79	BUSINESS ADMINISTRATION	S	3			▶			
1	GUILDHALL UNIVERSITY	□◆	55	79	BUSINESS AND FINANCE - HND	S	2			▶	1287	148	11
1	GUILDHALL UNIVERSITY	□◆	55	79	BUSINESS STUDIES	S	4			14	1988	160	8
1	GUILDHALL UNIVERSITY	□◆	55	79	EUROPEAN BUSINESS STUDIES	S	4	L		▶			
1	KINGSTON UNIVERSITY	□◆	69	28	BUSINESS STUDIES (EUROPEAN PROGRAMME)	S	4	L		18	383	13	3
1	KINGSTON UNIVERSITY	□◆	69	28	BUSINESS AND FINANCE - HND	S	2			EE-DD	758	82	11
1	KINGSTON UNIVERSITY	□◆	69	28	BUSINESS ADMINISTRATION	S	1/2	‡		▶	NEW		
1	KINGSTON UNIVERSITY	□◆	69	28	APPLIED PHYSICS & BUSINESS ADMIN.	J	3 4			6		3	
1	KINGSTON UNIVERSITY	□◆	69	28	CHEMISTRY WITH BUSINESS ADMINISTRATION	S	3 4	‡		8	98	13	14

				Institution	Course								
1	✱◆	N/A	N/A	LONDON INSTITUTE	BUSINESS STUDIES - HND	S	2		‡				
1	☐◆	91	3	MIDDLESEX UNIVERSITY	ELECTRONICS & BUSINESS STUDIES	S	3	4	+	8			
1	☐◆	91	3	MIDDLESEX UNIVERSITY	BUSINESS ADMINISTRATION	S	3			14			
1	☐◆	91	3	MIDDLESEX UNIVERSITY	BUSINESS STUDIES	S		4		14			
1	☐◆	91	3	MIDDLESEX UNIVERSITY	EUROPEAN BUSINESS ADMIN.:GER,FRA	S	4		L	16			
1	☐◆	35	55	NORTH LONDON UNIVERSITY	BUSINESS AND FINANCE	S	2			14-6			
1	☐◆	35	55	NORTH LONDON UNIVERSITY	CHEMISTRY WITH BUSINESS STUDIES	S	3	4 *		8			
1	☐◆	35	55	NORTH LONDON UNIVERSITY	BUSINESS STUDIES	S		4		BC-CCE			
1	✱◆	35	55	Q.M. & W. COLL, UNIV. OF LONDON	COMPUTER SCIENCE WITH BUSINESS STUDIES	S	3		‡	BCC	NEW		
1	✱◆	35	55	Q.M. & W. COLL, UNIV. OF LONDON	PHYSICS WITH BUSINESS STUDIES	S	3		‡	CCC			
1	✱◆	35	55	Q.M. & W. COLL, UNIV. OF LONDON	FRENCH, GERMAN WITH BUSINESS STUDIES	S	4		‡	18			
1	✱◆	35	55	Q.M. & W. COLL, UNIV. OF LONDON	BIOLOGICAL SCIENCES WITH BUS. STUDIES	S	3		‡	CCD			
1	✱◆	35	55	Q.M. & W. COLL, UNIV. OF LONDON	CIV ENG WITH BS (BSc Eng/BEng)	S	3		‡	CCC			
1	✱◆	35	55	Q.M. & W. COLL, UNIV. OF LONDON	CHEMISTRY WITH BUSINESS STUDIES	S	3		‡	18			
1	✱◆	35	55	Q.M. & W. COLL, UNIV. OF LONDON	MATHS WITH BUSINESS STUDIES	S	3		‡	BCC			
1	✱◆	N/A	N/A	ROEHAMPTION INSTITUTE	23 COMBINED OPTIONS/ & BUS. STUDIES 5	J	3/4						
1	☐◆	69	19	SOUTH BANK UNIVERSITY	BUSINESS AND FINANCE - HND	S	2	3	‡	D	845	182	22
1	☐◆	69	19	SOUTH BANK UNIVERSITY	BUSINESS STUDIES WITH LANGUAGES	S	3	4	L	CC-CD	1		
1	☐◆	69	19	SOUTH BANK UNIVERSITY	BUSINESS STUDIES	S	3	4		CCD	1145	117	10
1	☐◆	63	24	THAMES VALLEY UNIVERSITY	BUSINESS AND FINANCE - HND	S	2	3		8	3	1	33
1	☐◆	63	24	THAMES VALLEY UNIVERSITY	EUROPEAN BUSINESS STUDIES	S	3			16	163	6	4
1	☐◆	63	24	THAMES VALLEY UNIVERSITY	BUSINESS ADMINISTRATION	S	3			16			
1	☐◆	63	24	THAMES VALLEY UNIVERSITY	INTERNATIONAL BUSINESS STUDIES	S	3			▼	NEW		
1	☐◆	63	24	THAMES VALLEY UNIVERSITY	BUSINESS STUDIES	S	3	4		16	421	42	10
1	☐◆	63	24	THAMES VALLEY UNIVERSITY	BUSINESS AND FINANCE (BS) - HND	S	2	3		8	647	62	10
1	☐◆	63	24	THAMES VALLEY UNIVERSITY	BUSINESS AND TECHNOLOGY	S	3	4		▼			
1	✱◆	N/A	N/A	WEST LONDON INSTITUTE	BUSINESS STUDIES (& 9 MOD OPT) 6	J	3		‡				
1	✱◆	N/A	N/A	WEST LONDON INSTITUTE	BUSINESS AND FINANCE - HND	S	2		‡	12			

TABLE B – BUSINESS STUDIES COURSES (Continued)

	COLLEGE DETAILS				COURSE DETAILS						ENTRY		
REGION	NAME	TYPE	VALUE ADDED	EMPLOYMENT	SUBJECT	TYPE	DURATION	SANDWICH	SUBJECTS REQ	GRADES REQ	APPLY	GET ON	%
1	WEST LONDON INSTITUTE	✳◆	N/A	N/A	BUSINESS STUDIES WITH ART	S	3	‡		12			
1	WEST LONDON INSTITUTE	✳◆	N/A	N/A	BUSINESS STUDIES WITH FILM & T.V STUDIES	S	3	‡		12			
1	WEST LONDON INSTITUTE	✳◆	N/A	N/A	BUSINESS STUDIES WITH COMPUTER STUDIES	S	3	‡		12			
1	WESTMINSTER UNIVERSITY	□◆	91	10	BUSINESS STUDIES	S	4	‡		12	1983	167	8
1	WESTMINSTER UNIVERSITY	□◆	91	10	BUSINESS AND FINANCE - HND	S	2	‡		DE	1264	75	6
1	WESTMINSTER UNIVERSITY	□◆	91	10	INTERNATIONAL BUSINESS	S	4	‡		CC	465	46	10
1	WESTMINSTER UNIVERSITY	□◆	91	10	BUSINESS STUDIES (SERVICES)	S	3	‡		12	258	38	15
2	BOURNEMOUTH UNIVERSITY	□◆	55	34	BUSINESS AND FINANCE (TOURISM) - HND	S	2	▶		6 Approx			
2	BOURNEMOUTH UNIVERSITY	□◆	55	34	BUSINESS STUDIES	S	4	▶		16-14			
2	BOURNEMOUTH UNIVERSITY	□◆	55	34	BUSINESS AND FINANCE - HND	S	2	▶		6 Approx			
2	BRIGHTON UNIVERSITY	□◆	47	12	INTERNATIONAL BUSINESS	S	4	‡		18			1
2	BRIGHTON UNIVERSITY	□◆	47	12	BUSINESS AND FINANCE - HND	S	2	‡		8	929	122	13
2	BRIGHTON UNIVERSITY	□◆	47	12	BUSINESS STUDIES	S	4	‡		18	1634	116	7
2	BRIGHTON UNIVERSITY	□◆	47	12	FASH, TEXT & DESIGN WITH BUSINESS STUDIES	S	4						
2	CANTERBURY CHRISTCHURCH COLL	✳◆	N/A	N/A	BUSINESS STUDIES (& 28 COMB OPT) 14	J	3						
2	FARNBOROUGH COLLEGE	✳◆	N/A	N/A	BUSINESS ADMINISTRATION	S	3			12			
2	FARNBOROUGH COLLEGE	✳◆	N/A	N/A	BUS. AND FINANCE (FINANCIAL SERV) - HND	S	2			2	NEW		
2	FARNBOROUGH COLLEGE	✳◆	N/A	N/A	BUSINESS AND FINANCE (MKT,PER,FIN) - HND	S	2		3	2	235	140	60
2	FARNBOROUGH COLLEGE	✳◆	N/A	N/A	BUSINESS AND FINANCE - (EUR BUS) - HND	S	2		3	2	85	44	52
2	NORTH EAST SURREY COLLEGE	✳	N/A	N/A	EUROPEAN BUSINESS STUDIES - HND	S	2						
2	PORTSMOUTH UNIVERSITY	□◆	61	14	BUSINESS STUDIES WITH LANGAUGE	S	4	L		18	288	17	6

	Institution				Course								
2	PORTSMOUTH UNIVERSITY	□◆	61	14	BUSINESS AND FINANCE - HND	S	2	5*	‡	8	761	130	17
2	PORTSMOUTH UNIVERSITY	□◆	61	14	EXTENDED BUSINESS	S	4	5*	‡	▶	1	1	100
2	READING UNIVERSITY	◆◆	85	55	INTNL MANAGEMENT AND BUS ADMIN	S	4		‡	BBB	300	6	2
2	READING UNIVERSITY	◆◆	85	55	MANAGEMENT & BUSINESS ADMINISTRATION	S	3			BBB	723	12	2
2	SOUTHAMPTON INSTITUTE	✳◆	N/A	N/A	ELECTRONICS WITH BUSINESS	S	3		+&Sc	DD	28	8	29
2	SOUTHAMPTON INSTITUTE	✳◆	N/A	N/A	ECONOMICS WITH BUSINESS (FOUND YR)	S	4			D			
2	SOUTHAMPTON INSTITUTE	✳◆	N/A	N/A	BUSINESS AND FINANCE - HND	S	2			6	576	230	40
2	SOUTHAMPTON INSTITUTE	✳◆	N/A	N/A	BUSINESS AND LAW	S	3			10			
2	SOUTHAMPTON INSTITUTE	✳◆	N/A	N/A	BUSINESS ADMINISTRATION	S	3			10	26	54	208
2	SOUTHAMPTON INSTITUTE	✳◆	N/A	N/A	BUSINESS STUDIES	S	4			10	546	269	49
2	WYE COLLEGE, UNIV. OF LONDON	✳◆	N/A	N/A	BUS. STUDIES (EUROPEAN FOOD INDUSTRY)	S	4			14	11	1	9
3	BATH UNIVERSITY	◆◆	26	24	BUSINESS ADMINISTRATION	S	4			BBB	807	93	12
3	BRISTOL UNIVERSITY (UWE)	◆◆	35	30	INTERNATIONAL BUSINESS	S	4			CCC-BB	503	58	12
3	BRISTOL UNIVERSITY (UWE)	◆◆	35	30	BUSINESS AND FINANCE (MKTING PROG) - HND	S	2	3		8 Approx	899	75	8
3	BRISTOL UNIVERSITY (UWE)	◆◆	35	30	BUSINESS STUDIES	S	4		‡	CCC-BB	2054	164	8
3	BRISTOL UNIVERSITY (UWE)	◆◆	35	30	BUSINESS ADMINISTRATION	S	1		‡	▶	NEW		
3	BRISTOL UNIVERSITY (UWE)	◆◆	35	30	BUSINESS IN SCIENCE	S	4	1 Sc		14			
3	BRISTOL UNIVERSITY (UWE)	◆◆	35	30	BUSINESS AND FINANCE (TOUR PROG) - HND	S	2	3		8 Approx	662	52	8
3	BRISTOL UNIVERSITY (UWE)	◆◆	35	30	BUSINESS AND FINANCE (B.I.S. PROG) - HND	S	2	3		8 Approx	244	38	16
3	BRISTOL UNIVERSITY (UWE)	◆◆	35	30	BUSINESS STUDIES WITH TOURISM	S	1		‡	▶	7	1	14
3	CHELTENHAM & GLOUCESTER COLL	✳◆	N/A	N/A	BUSINESS STUDIES (& 23 MOD OPT) 17	S	3/4			▶			
3	CHELTENHAM & GLOUCESTER COLL	✳◆	N/A	N/A	BUSINESS AND FINANCE - HND	S	2			4			
3	PLYMOUTH UNIVERSITY	□◆	55	34	BUSINESS STUDIES WITH FR, GER, SP	S	4	L		CCD			
3	PLYMOUTH UNIVERSITY	□◆	55	34	LAW WITH BUSINESS STUDIES	S	3		‡	4			
3	PLYMOUTH UNIVERSITY	□◆	55	34	INTERNATIONAL BUSINESS	S	4		‡	CCD			
3	PLYMOUTH UNIVERSITY	□◆	55	34	INTERNATIONAL BUSINESS WITH FR,GER,IT,SP	S	4	L		CCD			
3	PLYMOUTH UNIVERSITY	□◆	55	34	BUSINESS & FINANCE (RETAILING) - HND	S	2		‡	6 Approx			
3	PLYMOUTH UNIVERSITY	□◆	55	34	GEOLOGY WITH BUSINESS	S	3			▶			

TABLE B – BUSINESS STUDIES COURSES (Continued)

	COLLEGE DETAILS				COURSE DETAILS				ENTRY				
REGION	NAME	VALUE ADDED	TYPE	EMPLOYMENT	SUBJECT	TYPE	DURATION	SANDWICH	SUBJECTS REQ	GRADES REQ	APPLY	GET ON	%
3	PLYMOUTH UNIVERSITY	55	□◆	34	BIOLOGY WITH BUSINESS (6 OPT) 19	S	3	‡		CCD/AB/BB			
3	PLYMOUTH UNIVERSITY	55	□◆	34	FISHERIES SCIENCE & BUS. STUDIES (10 OPT)	S	3	‡		NEW			
3	PLYMOUTH UNIVERSITY	55	□◆	34	BUSINESS & FINANCE (TRAV, TOUR OPT) - HND	S	2	‡		6 Approx			
3	PLYMOUTH UNIVERSITY	55	□◆	34	BUSINESS AND FINANCE - HND	S	2	‡		▶			
3	PLYMOUTH UNIVERSITY	55	□◆	34	BUSINESS STUDIES	S	3	4		CCD			
3	PLYMOUTH UNIVERSITY	55	□◆	34	MARITIME BUSINESS (5 OPT)	S	3	‡		NEW			
4	ASTON UNIVERSITY	78	◆◇	19	BUS ADMIN/PUBLIC POLICY & MANAGEMENT	J	3	4		20			
4	ASTON UNIVERSITY	78	◆◇	19	BUSINESS ADMINISTRATION/FRENCH,GERMAN	J	4			20			
4	ASTON UNIVERSITY	78	◆◇	19	BUSINESS ADMINISTRATION/MATHS	J	3	4		20			
4	ASTON UNIVERSITY	78	◆◇	19	CHEMISTRY/BUSINESS ADMINISTRATION	J	3	4		20			
4	ASTON UNIVERSITY	78	◆◇	19	BIOLOGY/BUSINESS ADMINISTRATION	J	3	4		20			
4	ASTON UNIVERSITY	78	◆◇	19	BUSINESS ADMIN./COMPUTER SCIENCE	J	3	4		20			
4	ASTON UNIVERSITY	78	◆◇	19	INTERNATIONAL BUSINESS/FRENCH,GERMAN	J	4			BBB-BBC			
4	ASTON UNIVERSITY	78	◆◇	19	MATERIALS/BUSINESS ADMINISTRATION	J	3	4		20			
4	ASTON UNIVERSITY	78	◆◇	19	SOCIAL STUDIES/BUSINESS ADMINISTRATION	J	3	4		20			
4	ASTON UNIVERSITY	78	◆◇	19	PSYCHOLOGY/BUSINESS ADMINISTRATION	J	3	4		20			
4	BEDFORD COLLEGE	N/A	◆◇	N/A	BUSINESS AND FINANCE - HND	S							
4	BEDFORD COLLEGE	N/A	◆◇	N/A	BUSINESS STUDIES (& 22 MOD OPT) 7	S	3	‡		14-12			
4	BIRMINGHAM UNIVERSITY	85	◆◇	67	BCom WITH ITALIAN	S	4	‡		BBC			
4	BIRMINGHAM UNIVERSITY	85	◆◇	67	BCom HONS	S	3			BBC	497	51	10
4	BIRMINGHAM UNIVERSITY	85	◆◇	67	BCom WITH GERMAN	S	4	L		BBC			

4	BIRMINGHAM UNIVERSITY	♦◆	85	67	MECH. ENGINEERING AND BUSINESS STUDIES	S	4	‡	BCC	541	82	15
4	BIRMINGHAM UNIVERSITY	♦◆	85	67	CHEMISTRY WITH BUSINESS STUDIES	S	3	+	CCC	431	82	19
4	BIRMINGHAM UNIVERSITY	♦◆	85	67	MANUF ENG & BUSINESS STUDIES	S	4	‡	CCC	246	73	30
4	BIRMINGHAM UNIVERSITY	♦◆	85	67	LAW WITH BUSINESS STUDIES	S	4	3 +	28-24			
4	BIRMINGHAM UNIVERSITY	♦◆	85	67	BCom WITH FRENCH	S	4	L	BBB			
4	BIRMINGHAM UNIVERSITY	♦◆	85	67	BCom(RUSS) HONS	S	3	‡	BBC			
4	BIRMINGHAM UNIVERSITY	♦◆	85	67	BCom WITH SPANISH	S	4	‡	BBC			
4	BIRMINGHAM UNIVERSITY	♦◆	85	67	BUSINESS STUDIES/PORTUGESE	J	4		BBC			
4	BUCKINGHAM UNIVERSITY	♦◆	46	1	BUS. STUDIES - INTL. HOTEL MANAGEMENT	S	3		16	171	7	4
4	BUCKINGHAM UNIVERSITY	♦◆	46	1	PSYCHOLOGY WITH BUSINESS STUDIES	S	2		12	55	5	9
4	BUCKINGHAM UNIVERSITY	♦◆	46	1	COMPUTER SCIENCE WITH BUSINESS STUDIES	S	2		12	42	1	2
4	BUCKINGHAM UNIVERSITY	♦◆	46	1	BUSINESS STUDIES	S	2		16	401	31	8
4	BUCKINGHAMSHIRE COLLEGE	❋◆	N/A	N/A	BUSINESS AND FINANCE - HND	S	2	‡	DE	403	175	43
4	BUCKINGHAMSHIRE COLLEGE	❋◆	N/A	N/A	INTERNATIONAL BUSINESS ADMINISTRATION	S	4	‡	CC	127	29	23
4	BUCKINGHAMSHIRE COLLEGE	❋◆	N/A	N/A	EUROPEAN BUSINESS STUDIES WITH SPANISH	S	4	‡	CC	95	16	17
4	BUCKINGHAMSHIRE COLLEGE	❋◆	N/A	N/A	EUROPEAN BUSINESS STUDIES WITH ITALIAN	S	4	‡	CC	84	15	18
4	BUCKINGHAMSHIRE COLLEGE	❋◆	N/A	N/A	EUROPEAN BUSINESS STUDIES WITH GERMAN	S	4	L	CC	82	12	15
4	BUCKINGHAMSHIRE COLLEGE	❋◆	N/A	N/A	BUSINESS STUDIES	S	1	‡		302	65	22
4	BUCKINGHAMSHIRE COLLEGE	❋◆	N/A	N/A	BUSINESS ADMINISTRATION	S	4	‡	CC	157	127	81
4	BUCKINGHAMSHIRE COLLEGE	❋◆	N/A	N/A	EUROPEAN BUSINESS STUDIES WITH FRENCH	S	4	L	CC	207	26	13
4	BUCKINGHAMSHIRE COLLEGE	❋◆	N/A	N/A	BUSINESS ADMINISTRATION WTH ENVIR MGT	S	3	‡	DD	45	28	62
4	CENTRAL ENGLAND UNIVERSITY	♦◆	53	14	BUSINESS ADMINISTRATION & ENTERPRISE	S	1		▼			
4	CENTRAL ENGLAND UNIVERSITY	♦◆	53	14	BUSINESS AND FINANCE - HND	S	2	3	8	1229	126	10
4	CENTRAL ENGLAND UNIVERSITY	♦◆	53	14	BUSINESS STUDIES	S	4		CCD-CC	1785	118	7
4	COVENTRY UNIVERSITY	□◆	47	18	LAW AND BUSINESS STUDIES	S	3	4	18			
4	COVENTRY UNIVERSITY	□◆	47	18	BUSINESS AND FINANCE - HND	S	2		8	963	117	12
4	COVENTRY UNIVERSITY	□◆	47	18	BUSINESS ADMINISTRATION	S	3	‡	14	106		
4	COVENTRY UNIVERSITY	□◆	47	18	BUSINESS STUDIES	S	4	‡	16	1165	63	5

TABLE B – BUSINESS STUDIES COURSES (Continued)

REGION	NAME	TYPE	VALUE ADDED	EMPLOYMENT	SUBJECT	TYPE	DURATION	SANDWICH	SUBJECTS REQ	GRADES REQ	APPLY	GET ON	%
4	COVENTRY UNIVERSITY	□◆	47	18	EUROPEAN BUSINESS AND TECHNOLOGY	S	4			14	358	116	32
4	COVENTRY UNIVERSITY	□◆	47	18	EUROPEAN BUSINESS STUDIES	S	3	‡		16	465	16	3
4	COVENTRY UNIVERSITY	□◆	47	18	STATISTICS AND BUSINESS STUDIES	S	4						
4	COVENTRY UNIVERSITY	□◆	47	18	INTERNATIONAL STUDIES AND BUS. STUD.	S	3			14	119	13	11
4	CRANFIELD UNIVERSITY	●	N/A	N/A	BUSINESS AND FINANCE - HND	S	2	‡		E			
4	DE MONTFORT UNIVERSITY	□◆	79	2	PHYSICS WITH BUSINESS STUDIES	S	4			12-8	86	12	14
4	DE MONTFORT UNIVERSITY	□❖	79	2	CHEMISTRY WITH BUSINESS STUDIES (EXT)	S	5	‡		8-4	NEW		
4	DE MONTFORT UNIVERSITY	□◆	79	2	BUSINESS STUDIES	S	4			18	1820	172	9
4	DE MONTFORT UNIVERSITY	□◆	79	2	BUSINESS ADMINISTRATION	S	3			14-12			
4	DE MONTFORT UNIVERSITY	□◆	79	2	PHYSICS WITH BUSINESS STUDIES (EXT)	S	5			8-4	38	23	61
4	DE MONTFORT UNIVERSITY	□❖	79	2	BIOMEDICAL SCIENCES WITH BUS. STUDIES	S	4			12			
4	DE MONTFORT UNIVERSITY	□◆	79	2	CHEMISTRY WITH BUSINESS STUDIES	S	4			12-8	138	24	17
4	DE MONTFORT UNIVERSITY	□◆	79	2	BUSINESS AND FINANCE - HND	S	2			6	1231	180	15
4	DERBY UNIVERSITY	□◆	69	90	BUSINESS STUDIES	S	4			14	483	126	26
4	DERBY UNIVERSITY	□◆	69	90	BUSINESS ADMINISTRATION	S	3			12	36	16	44
4	DERBY UNIVERSITY	□◆	69	90	BUSINESS AND FINANCE - HND	S	2			4	523	371	71
4	DERBY UNIVERSITY	□◆	69	90	MODERN TECHNOLOGY & BUSINESS ADMIN	S	3	‡		4	NEW		
4	DERBY UNIVERSITY	□◆	69	90	BUSINESS AND FINANCE (EUR STREAM) - HND	S	2	‡		4	174	74	43
4	EDGE HILL COLLEGE	❋◆	N/A	N/A	BUSINESS STUDIES - HND	S	2	‡			60	12	20
4	HARPER ADAMS AGRICULTURAL CO	✱	N/A	N/A	AGRI-FOOD FOOD MARKETING & BUS STUDIES	S	4			8			
4	HARPER ADAMS AGRICULTURAL CO	✱	N/A	N/A	AGRIC MARKETING & BUS STUDIES - HND	S	3			2			

				Institution	Course							
4	●◆	4	67	KEELE UNIVERSITY	BUSINESS ADMINISTRATION+(5 SOC SCI OPT) 8	J	3/4					
4	●◆	4	67	KEELE UNIVERSITY	GERMAN/RUSSIAN & BUSINESS ADMIN.	J	3/4	‡	BBC			
4	●◆	4	67	KEELE UNIVERSITY	FRENCH/GERMAN & BUSINESS ADMIN.	J	3/4	‡	BBC			
4	●◆	41	34	LOUGHBOROUGH UNIVERSITY	MATERIALS WITH BUSINESS STUDIES	S	3	4	*	CDD	276	19	7
4	●◆	41	34	LOUGHBOROUGH UNIVERSITY	EUROPEAN BUSINESS	S	4	L	BBC	309	30	10
4	❋◆	N/A	N/A	LUTON COLLEGE OF H.E.	BUSINESS STUDIES	S	4	‡	10	504	131	26
4	❋◆	N/A	N/A	LUTON COLLEGE OF H.E.	BUSINESS ADMINISTRATION	S	3	‡	10			
4	❋◆	N/A	N/A	LUTON COLLEGE OF H.E.	BUSINESS AND FINANCE - HND	S	2	‡	4			
4	❋◆	N/A	N/A	LUTON COLLEGE OF H.E.	BUSINESS STUDIES (1 YR CONV TO DEG)	S	1	‡				
4	❋◆	N/A	N/A	LUTON COLLEGE OF H.E.	FOUNDATION BUSINESS	S	4 *	‡				
4	❋◆	N/A	N/A	MATTHEW BOULTON COLLEGE	BUSINESS STUDIES - HND	S	2			50	20	40
4	❋◆	N/A	N/A	NENE COLLEGE	BUSINESS STUDIES	S	4		CC-CDD	389	106	27
4	❋◆	N/A	N/A	NENE COLLEGE	EUROPEAN BUS. STUDIES FR,GER,IT,SPAN	S	4		CD(S)			
4	❋◆	N/A	N/A	NENE COLLEGE	COMBINED STUDIES WITH BUSINESS ADMIN	J	3		10	242	75	31
4	❋◆	N/A	N/A	NENE COLLEGE	BUSINESS & FINANCE - HND	S	2		2	399	125	31
4	□◆	31	14	NOTTINGHAM TRENT UNIVERSITY	EUROPEAN BUSINESS WTH FR,GER,SPAN	S	4	‡	14			
4	□◆	31	14	NOTTINGHAM TRENT UNIVERSITY	BUSINESS STUDIES	S	4	‡	CCD	3806	74	2
4	□◆	31	14	NOTTINGHAM TRENT UNIVERSITY	BUSINESS AND FINANCE	S	2	3	‡	▼	1926	60	3
4	□◆	31	14	NOTTINGHAM TRENT UNIVERSITY	BUSINESS ADMINISTRATION	S	3	‡	▼	NEW		
4	□◆	31	14	NOTTINGHAM TRENT UNIVERSITY	BUSINESS & QUALITY MANAGEMENT	S	4	‡	12	240	20	8
4	□◆	31	12	OXFORD BROOKES UNIVERSITY	EUROPEAN BUSINESS STUDIES	S	4	‡				
4	□◆	31	12	OXFORD BROOKES UNIVERSITY	BUS ADMIN & MANAGEMENT (40 MOD OPT)18	J	3					
4	●◆	63	47	STAFFORDSHIRE UNIVERSITY	MANUF ENG WITH BUSINESS STUDIES (EXT)	S	4	5		4			
4	●◆	63	47	STAFFORDSHIRE UNIVERSITY	MANUFACTURING ENGINEERING WITH B.S.	S	3	4	‡	12			
4	●◆	63	47	STAFFORDSHIRE UNIVERSITY	BUSINESS ADMINISTRATION & ENVIR	S	3		DD			
4	●◆	63	47	STAFFORDSHIRE UNIVERSITY	MANU ENG WITH BUS. STUD. (EXT) - HND	S	3		2			
4	●◆	63	47	STAFFORDSHIRE UNIVERSITY	BUSINESS STUDIES & (14 MOD OPT) 10	J	3					
4	●◆	63	47	STAFFORDSHIRE UNIVERSITY	BUSINESS STUDIES	S	4		16			

TABLE B – BUSINESS STUDIES COURSES (Continued)

REGION	NAME	TYPE	VALUE ADDED	EMPLOYMENT	SUBJECT	TYPE	DURATION	SANDWICH	SUBJECTS REQ	GRADES REQ	APPLY	%	% GET ON
4	STAFFORDSHIRE UNIVERSITY	◆◆	63	47	BUSINESS AND INNOVATION	S	3			DD	87	8	9
4	STAFFORDSHIRE UNIVERSITY	◆◆	63	47	BUSINESS & ENVIRONMENTAL TECHNOLOGY	S	3			DD			
4	STAFFORDSHIRE UNIVERSITY	◆◆	63	47	BUSINESS AND FINANCE - HND	S	2	3		2			
4	STAFFORDSHIRE UNIVERSITY	◆◆	63	47	BUSINESS STUDIES WITH TOURISM	S	3	4		16			
4	STAFFORDSHIRE UNIVERSITY	◆◆	63	47	MANU ENG WITH BS - HND	S	2			2			
4	WARWICK UNIVERSITY	◆◆	19	55	MATHEMATICS & BUSINESS STUDIES	S	3			AAB	49	4	8
4	WARWICK UNIVERSITY	◆◆	19	55	COMPUTER SCIENCE & BUSINESS STUDIES	S	3			BBB			
4	WARWICK UNIVERSITY	◆◆	19	55	INTERNATIONAL BUSINESS	S	4	L		BBB			
4	WARWICK UNIVERSITY	◆◆	19	55	APPLIED MATHEMATICS & BUSINESS STUDIES	S	3/4			AAB	13		
4	WARWICK UNIVERSITY	◆◆	19	55	PHYSICS & BUSINESS STUDIES	S	3			BCC	25	4	16
4	WARWICK UNIVERSITY	◆◆	19	55	GERMAN & BUSINESS STUDIES	S	4	L		BBB			
4	WARWICK UNIVERSITY	◆◆	19	55	CHEMISTRY & BUSINESS STUDIES	S	3/4			CCD	108	21	19
4	WARWICK UNIVERSITY	◆◆	19	55	ENGINEERING WITH BUSINESS STUDIES	S	3			BCC	106	9	8
4	WOLVERHAMPTON UNIVERSITY	◆◆	91	50	BUSINESS AND FINANCE - HND	S	2	‡		6 Approx			
4	WOLVERHAMPTON UNIVERSITY	◆◆	91	50	BUSINESS & MANUFACTURING SYSTEMS	S	4	▼					
4	WOLVERHAMPTON UNIVERSITY	◆◆	91	50	EUROPEAN BUSINESS STUDIES	S	4			16			
4	WOLVERHAMPTON UNIVERSITY	◆◆	91	50	BUSINESS STUDIES	S	4	▼	‡	▼			
4	WOLVERHAMPTON UNIVERSITY	◆◆	91	50	LANGUAGES, BUS. AND INFO TECHNOLOGY	S	3	‡		▼			
5	ANGLIA POLY UNIVERSITY	✱◆	53	8	BUSINESS STUDIES (EUR MKTING) - HND	S				▼			
5	ANGLIA POLY UNIVERSITY	✱◆	53	8	BUSINESS STUDIES	S	4			12	647	81	13
5	ANGLIA POLY UNIVERSITY	✱◆	53	8	BUS STUDIES (PERSONNEL MANYMENT) - HND	S	2	‡		4	144	12	8

				Institution	Course				Offer			
5	✳◆	53	8	ANGLIA POLY UNIVERSITY	BUSINESS STUDIES (COMPANY ADMIN) - HND	S	2	†	4	30	4	13
5	✳◆	53	8	ANGLIA POLY UNIVERSITY	EUROPEAN BUSINESS ADMINISTRATION	S	4	†	12	156	40	26
5	✳◆	53	8	ANGLIA POLY UNIVERSITY	BUS. STUDIES (BUSINESS & FINANCE) - HND	S	2	†	4	490	125	26
5	✳◆	53	8	ANGLIA POLY UNIVERSITY	BUS STUDIES (EURO BUSINESS ADMIN) - HND	S	2	†	4	87	11	13
5	✳◆	53	8	ANGLIA POLY UNIVERSITY	BUSINESS STUDIES (LEISURE STUDIES) - HND	S	2	†	4	NEW		
5	✳◆	53	8	ANGLIA POLY UNIVERSITY	BUSINESS STUDIES (MKTING) - HND	S	2	†	4	224	26	12
5	✳◆	N/A	N/A	CITY COLLEGE, NORWICH	BUSINESS AND FINANCE - HND	S	2		E			
5	✳◆	N/A	N/A	COLCHESTER INSTITUTE	BUSINESS STUDIES - HND	S	2		6 Approx			
5	✳◆	N/A	N/A	COLCHESTER INSTITUTE	BUSINESS STUDIES (CATERING MGT)	S	4					
5	●◆	10	79	ESSEX UNIVERSITY	TECHNOLOGICAL PHYSICS WITH BUS STUDIES	S	4		CDD	37	10	27
5	●◆	10	79	ESSEX UNIVERSITY	CHEMISTRY WITH EUROPEAN BUS. STUDIES	S	4		BBC	22	9	41
5	●◆	79	3	HERTFORDSHIRE UNIVERSITY	BUSINESS STUDIES	S	4		16	956	86	9
5	●◆	79	3	HERTFORDSHIRE UNIVERSITY	BUSINESS STUDIES - HND	S	2	†	8 Approx			
5	●◆	79	3	HERTFORDSHIRE UNIVERSITY	EUROPEAN BUSINESS STUDIES	S	4	†	16	475	70	15
5	●◆	79	3	HERTFORDSHIRE UNIVERSITY	BUSINESS AND FINANCE - HND	S	2		10-8	840	82	10
5	●◆	79	3	HERTFORDSHIRE UNIVERSITY	MODULAR BUSINESS DEGREE	S	3	†	8			
5	●◆	47	62	HULL UNIVERSITY	BUSINESS STUDIES	S	3		BBB	1395	36	3
5	●◆	47	62	HULL UNIVERSITY	BUSINESS STUDIES/DU,FR,GER,SCAN,SP	J	4	†	BBB			
5	●◆	47	62	HULL UNIVERSITY	BUSINESS STUDIES/ITALIAN	J	4	†	BBB-BCC			
5	□◆	79	55	HUMBERSIDE UNIVERSITY	EUROPEAN BUS. STUDIES/SCANDANAVIAN	S	4	L		NEW		
5	□◆	79	55	HUMBERSIDE UNIVERSITY	EUROPEAN BUSINESS STUDIES/GERMAN	S	4	L	16	168	13	8
5	□◆	79	55	HUMBERSIDE UNIVERSITY	EUROPEAN BUSINESS STUDIES/SPANISH	S	4	L	16	125	6	5
5	□◆	79	55	HUMBERSIDE UNIVERSITY	BUSINESS STUDIES - HND	S	2		6	1246	331	27
5	□◆	79	55	HUMBERSIDE UNIVERSITY	INTERNATIONAL BUSINESS STUDIES	S		L	10			
5	□◆	79	55	HUMBERSIDE UNIVERSITY	EUROPEAN BUSINESS STUDIES/FRENCH	S	4	L	16	383	43	11
5	□◆	79	55	HUMBERSIDE UNIVERSITY	BUSINESS STUDIES	S	4		16	979	143	15
5	✳◆	N/A	N/A	SUFFOLK COLLEGE	BUSINESS AND FINANCE (7 MOD OPT) 15 - HND	S	2		6 Approx			
5	✳◆	N/A	N/A	SUFFOLK COLLEGE	BUSINESS ADMINISTRATION	S	ACC		8 Approx			

TABLE B – BUSINESS STUDIES COURSES (Continued)

REGION	NAME	COLLEGE DETAILS			COURSE DETAILS						ENTRY		
		TYPE	VALUE ADDED	EMPLOYMENT	SUBJECT	TYPE	DURATION	SANDWICH	SUBJECTS REQ	GRADES REQ	APPLY		% GET ON
5	SUFFOLK COLLEGE	**❖	N/A	N/A	BUSINESS STUDIES WITH (6 MOD OPT) 15	S	3			8 Approx			
5	WEST HERTS COLLEGE	**❖	N/A	N/A	BUSINESS ADMINISTRATION	S	1				NEW		
5	WEST HERTS COLLEGE	**❖	N/A	N/A	BUSINESS STUDIES - HND	S	2			6 Approx	134	86	64
6	ASKHAM BRYAN COLLAGE	**◆	N/A	N/A	BUSINESS AND FINANCE - HND	S	3	‡		▶			
6	BRADFORD AND IKLEY COLL	**❖	N/A	N/A	BUSINESS ADMIN (FRENCH OR GERMAN)	S	3	‡		8	352	117	33
6	BRADFORD AND IKLEY COLL	**❖	N/A	N/A	BUSINESS AND FINANCE - HND	S	2	‡		4	440	129	29
6	BRADFORD UNIVERSITY	●◆	91	50	BUSINESS AND MANAGEMENT STUDIES	S	3/4	‡		BBC	1734	129	7
6	DONCASTER COLLEGE	✳	N/A	N/A	BUSINESS STUDIES	S	4			12			
6	DONCASTER COLLEGE	✳	N/A	N/A	BUSINESS ADMINISTRATION	S	3			12			
6	DONCASTER COLLEGE	✳	N/A	N/A	BUSINESS AND FINANCE - HND	S	2			2			
6	HUDDERSFIELD UNIVERSITY	□◆	63	41	BUSINESS STUDIES WITH LANGUAGE	S	4			16	NEW		
6	HUDDERSFIELD UNIVERSITY	●◆	63	41	PHY WITH BUSINESS & MANAGEMENT	S	4			BBC-BCC	NEW		
6	HUDDERSFIELD UNIVERSITY	□◆	63	41	BUSINESS AND FINANCE - HND	S	2			DD	1147	205	18
6	HUDDERSFIELD UNIVERSITY	□◆	63	41	TECH:BUSINESS STUDIES(BEd)	S	2 Acc	‡					
6	HUDDERSFIELD UNIVERSITY	□◆	63	41	BUSINESS STUDIES	S	4			16	759	123	16
6	LEEDS METRO UNIVERSITY	□◆	91	8	BUSINESS AND FINANCE - HND	S	3			6 Approx	1650	88	5
6	LEEDS METRO UNIVERSITY	□◆	91	8	BUSINESS STUDIES	S	4			CCC-BB	2526	77	3
6	LEEDS METRO UNIVERSITY	□◆	91	8	APPLIED CHEMISTRY WITH BUSINESS STUDIES	S	4		1 Sc				4
6	NEW COLLEGE, DURHAM	**◆	N/A	N/A	BUSINESS AND FINANCE - HND	S	2	‡		2	920	206	22
6	NORTHUMBRIA UNIVERSITY	●◆	47	88	INTERNATIONAL BUSINESS AND TECHNOLOGY	S	5			E			
6	NORTHUMBRIA UNIVERSITY	●◆	47	88	SECRETARIAL & BUSINESS ADMINISTRATION	S	3			12	184	49	27

6	●◆	47	88	NORTHUMBRIA UNIVERSITY	INTERNATIONAL BUSINESS & TECHNOLOGY	S	4			DDD	70	15	21
6	●◆	47	88	NORTHUMBRIA UNIVERSITY	COMPUTING FOR BUSINESS	S	4			8	200	37	19
6	□◆	63	50	SHEFFIELD HALLAM UNIVERSITY	BUSINESS STUDIES (FULL TIME)	S	3		‡	14	1331	24	2
6	□◆	63	50	SHEFFIELD HALLAM UNIVERSITY	COMPUTING MATHEMATICS WITH BUS STUDIES	S	4		‡	▶			
6	□◆	63	50	SHEFFIELD HALLAM UNIVERSITY	INTERNATIONAL BUS./FR.,GER.,IT.,JAP,PO.SP	S	3/4		‡	16-14			
6	□◆	63	50	SHEFFIELD HALLAM UNIVERSITY	BUSINESS & FINANCE - HND	S	2			6	1834	102	6
6	□◆	63	50	SHEFFIELD HALLAM UNIVERSITY	BUSINESS STUDIES (SANDWICH)	S	4		‡	14	1873	142	8
6	●◆	10	47	SHEFFIELD UNIVERSITY	FR.,RUSS.,GER.,SP./BUSINESS STUDIES	S	4		L	BBC			
6	●◆	10	47	SHEFFIELD UNIVERSITY	BUSINESS STUDIES/JAPANESE STUDIES	S	4			BBB			
6	●◆	10	47	SHEFFIELD UNIVERSITY	BUSINESS STUDIES/ECONOMICS	S	3			BBB			
6	●◆	10	47	SHEFFIELD UNIVERSITY	BUSINESS STUDIES/INFORMATION MGT.	S	3			BBB	NEW		
6	●◆	10	47	SHEFFIELD UNIVERSITY	KOREAN/BUSINESS STUDIES	S				BBB	NEW		
6	●◆	10	47	SHEFFIELD UNIVERSITY	BUSINESS STUDIES AND ENG	J	3/4		+	BCC			
6	●◆	10	47	SHEFFIELD UNIVERSITY	BUSINESS STUDIES	S	3			BBB	2197	62	3
6	●◆	75	94	SUNDERLAND UNIVERSITY	FRENCH, GERMAN/BUSINESS STUDIES	J	4		L	8-6			
6	●◆	75	94	SUNDERLAND UNIVERSITY	BUSINESS STUDIES (SHORT)	S	2	2 Acc	‡	14			
6	●◆	75	94	SUNDERLAND UNIVERSITY	EUROPEAN BUSINESS STUDIES	S	4		‡	14			
6	●◆	75	94	SUNDERLAND UNIVERSITY	BUSINESS ADMINISTRATION	S	3		‡	14			
6	●◆	75	94	SUNDERLAND UNIVERSITY	BUSINESS STUDIES	S	4		‡	14	496	159	32
6	●◆	75	94	SUNDERLAND UNIVERSITY	(6 MOD OPT'Y & BUSINESS STUDIES 11	J	3		‡		NEW		
6	●◆	75	94	SUNDERLAND UNIVERSITY	BUSINESS & FINANCE - HND	S	2		‡	6	583	196	34
6	●◆	75	94	SUNDERLAND UNIVERSITY	ACCOUNTING & BUSINESS	S	3		‡	14	288	53	20
6	●◆	75	94	SUNDERLAND UNIVERSITY	BUSINESS ADMINISTRATION (SHORT)	S	2		‡	▶			
6	●◆	75	79	TEESSIDE UNIVERSITY	APP SC WITH BUSINESS	S	3						
6	●◆	75	79	TEESSIDE UNIVERSITY	BUSINESS STUDIES	S	4		‡	CCD			
6	●◆	75	79	TEESSIDE UNIVERSITY	BUSINESS & FINANCE - HND	S	2			8 Approx			
6	●◆	75	79	TEESSIDE UNIVERSITY	MANUFACTURING WITH BUSINESS	S	4						
6	●◆	75	79	TEESSIDE UNIVERSITY	INTERNATIONAL BUSINESS	S	4		‡	CCD			

TABLE B – BUSINESS STUDIES COURSES (Continued)

	COLLEGE DETAILS				COURSE DETAILS						ENTRY	
REGION	NAME	TYPE	VALUE ADDED	EMPLOYMENT	SUBJECT	TYPE	DURATION	SANDWICH	SUBJECTS REQ	GRADES REQ	APPLY	GET ON %
7	BOLTON INSTITUTE	■◆	N/A	N/A	BUSINESS ADMINISTRATION	S	3			14-10		
7	BOLTON INSTITUTE	■◆	N/A	N/A	BUSINESS STUDIES(& 20 COMB OPT) 9	J	3					
7	CENTRAL LANCS UNIVERSITY	●◆	41	92	INTERNATIONAL BUSINESS	S	3			18	NEW	
7	CENTRAL LANCS UNIVERSITY	●◆	41	92	BUSINESS & FINANCE - HND	S	2			DD	816 146	18
7	CENTRAL LANCS UNIVERSITY	●◆	41	92	BUSINESS STUDIES	S	4			CCC	990 56	6
7	CENTRAL LANCS UNIVERSITY	●◆	41	92	BUSINESS & FINANCE(BUS & ENVIR ST) - HND	S	2	‡		2	NEW	
7	CENTRAL LANCS UNIVERSITY	●◆	41	92	EUROPEAN BUSINESS ADMIN & LANGUAGE	S	3	L		CC-CCD	419 72	17
7	CENTRAL LANCS UNIVERSITY	●◆	41	92	BUSINESS & FINANCE(BUS INFO MGT) - HND	S	2	L		DD	816 146	18
7	L'POOL JOHN MOORES UNIVERSITY	□◆	69	30	SPORTS SCIENCE & BUSINESS	J	3	L		18-16		
7	L'POOL JOHN MOORES UNIVERSITY	□◆	69	30	BUSINESS & FINANCE - HND	S	2	L		10	1102 11	1
7	L'POOL JOHN MOORES UNIVERSITY	□◆	69	30	PRODUCTION DESIGN & BUSINESS	J	3	L		18-16		
7	L'POOL JOHN MOORES UNIVERSITY	□◆	69	30	LAW & BUSINESS	S	4	L		16		
7	L'POOL JOHN MOORES UNIVERSITY	□◆	69	30	BUSINESS & BUSINESS LAW	J	3	‡		18-16		
7	L'POOL JOHN MOORES UNIVERSITY	□◆	69	30	BUSINESS ADMINISTRATION	S	3	‡		18-16		
7	L'POOL JOHN MOORES UNIVERSITY	□◆	69	30	BUSINESS STUDIES	S	3 4	‡		18-16	1586 99	6
7	L'POOL JOHN MOORES UNIVERSITY	□◆	69	30	ECONOMICS & BUSINESS	J	3	‡		18-16		
7	L'POOL JOHN MOORES UNIVERSITY	□◆	69	30	PLANNING STUDIES & BUSINESS	J	3	L		18		
7	L'POOL JOHN MOORES UNIVERSITY	□◆	69	30	INTNL BUSINESS WITH FRENCH, GER, SP, JAP	S	3	L		18-16		
7	L'POOL JOHN MOORES UNIVERSITY	□◆	69	30	BUSINESS & APPLIED PSYCHOLOGY	J	3	‡		18-16		
7	MANCHESTER METRO UNIVERSITY	□◆	91	3	BUSINESS	S	4			BCC-AA	1078 117	11
7	MANCHESTER METRO UNIVERSITY	□◆	91	3	BUSINESS & FINANCE - HND	S	2			6 Approx	1619 91	6

No.	Institution	Mark			Course	J/S			Grade			
7	STOCKPORT COLLEGE	✳◆	N/A	N/A	BUSINESS & FINANCE - HND	S	2	‡	6 Approx			
7	S. MARTINS COLLGE	✳✳	N/A	N/A	GEOGRAPHY/BUSINESS & MANAGEMENT STUD.	J	3	‡	CC			
7	S. MARTINS COLLGE	✳✳	N/A	N/A	HISTORY/BUSINESS & MANAGEMENT STUDIES	J	3	‡	CC			
7	S. MARTINS COLLGE	✳◆	N/A	N/A	HEALTH PROMOTION/BUS & MGT STUDIES	J	3	‡	CC			
7	S. MARTINS COLLGE	✳◆	N/A	N/A	ENG/BUS & MANAGEMENT STUDIES	J	3	‡	BC			
7	UMIST	✳✳	75	62	INTL MGT W/AMERICAN BUS. ST. (3 YR ABR)	S	4		ABB	230	26	11
7	UNIVERSITY COLLEGE, SALFORD	✳✳	N/A	N/A	BUSINESS STUDIES	S	4		CC	237	56	24
7	UNIVERSITY COLLEGE, SALFORD	✳✳	N/A	N/A	BUSINESS & FINANCE (MARKETING) - HND	S	2		6 Approx	212	50	24
7	UNIVERSITY COLLEGE, SALFORD	✳◆	N/A	N/A	BUSINESS & FINANCE (PERSONNEL) - HND	S	2		6 Approx	157	33	21
7	UNIVERSITY COLLEGE, SALFORD	✳◆	N/A	N/A	BUSINESS & FINANCE (TOUR & MKTNG) - HND	S	2		6 Approx	NEW		
8	QUEEN'S UNIVERSITY BELFAST	◆◆	18	55	BUSINESS ADMIN & COMPUTER SCIENCE	J	3/4		CCC			
8	QUEEN'S UNIVERSITY BELFAST	◆◆	18	55	BUSINESS ADMIN/FRENCH,ITALIAN,SPANISH	J	4		BCC-CCC			
8	QUEEN'S UNIVERSITY BELFAST	◆◆	18	55	BUSINESS ADMINISTRATION/GERMAN	J	4	5	BCC-CCC			
8	ULSTER UNIVERSITY	◆◆	69	30	BUSINESS STUDIES WITH JAPANESE	S	4		BCC	143	42	29
8	ULSTER UNIVERSITY	◆◆	69	30	BUSINESS STUDIES WITH SPECIALISMS	S	4		BCC	NEW		
8	ULSTER UNIVERSITY	◆◆	69	30	BUSINESS STUDIES WITH COMPUTING	S	3/4		BCC	NEW		
8	ULSTER UNIVERSITY	◆◆	69	30	SCIENCE WITH BUSINESS STUDIES	S	4		CCD	101	12	12
8	ULSTER UNIVERSITY	◆◆	69	30	BUSINESS STUDIES	S	4		BBC	1695	83	5
8	ULSTER UNIVERSITY	◆◆	69	30	EUROPEAN BUSINESS STUDIES	S	4	L	BCC	710	67	9
9	CARDIFF INSTITUTE	✳✳	N/A	N/A	BUSINESS & FINANCE (ADMIN) - HND	S	2		6	362	48	13
9	CARDIFF INSTITUTE	✳◆	N/A	N/A	BUSINESS STUDIES	S	3		10	261	24	9
9	CARDIFF INSTITUTE	✳✳	N/A	N/A	BUSINESS STUDIES ADMIN	S	1	‡		175	4	2
9	CARDIFF INSTITUTE	✳◆	N/A	N/A	BUSINESS & FINANCE (TOUR) - HND	S	2		6	335	52	16
9	CARDIFF UNIVERSITY	◆◆	19	74	BUSINESS STUDIES WITH JAPANESE	S	4		BBC	847	110	13
9	CARDIFF UNIVERSITY	◆◆	19	74	BUSINESS ADMINISTRATION	S	3		BBC	NEW		
9	CARDIFF UNIVERSITY	◆◆	19	74	BUSINESS ADMIN. WITH FR,GER,ITAL,SP	S	4	L	BBC			
9	GLAMORGAN UNIVERSITY	◆◆	55	95	LANGUAGE & EUROPEAN BUS. ADMIN - HND	S	2		4	77	68	88
9	GLAMORGAN UNIVERSITY	◆◆	55	95	ELECTRONICS WITH EUROPEAN BUS. STUDIES	S	3	‡	8	1		

TABLE B – BUSINESS STUDIES COURSES (Continued)

	COLLEGE DETAILS			COURSE DETAILS							ENTRY		
REGION	NAME	TYPE	VALUE ADDED	EMPLOYMENT	SUBJECT	TYPE	DURATION	SANDWICH	SUBJECTS REQ	GRADES REQ	APPLY	GET ON	%
9	GLAMORGAN UNIVERSITY	●◆	55	95	TECHNOLOGY & BUSINESS STUDIES	S	3 4	‡		10			
9	GLAMORGAN UNIVERSITY	●◆	55	95	BUSINESS & FINANCE - HND	S	2			6	553	314	57
9	GLAMORGAN UNIVERSITY	●◆	55	95	EUROPEAN BUSINESS ADMINISTRATION	S	4			16-14	24		
9	GLAMORGAN UNIVERSITY	●◆	55	95	BUSINESS STUDIES	S	4			26-24	476	138	29
9	GWENT COLLEGE	●✦◆	N/A	N/A	BUSINESS ADMINISTRATION	S	3				54	28	52
9	GWENT COLLEGE	●✦◆	N/A	N/A	BUSINESS & FINANCE	S	2	‡			184	94	51
9	GWENT COLLEGE	●✦◆	N/A	N/A	EUROPEAN BUSINESS STUDIES - HND	S	2			6 Approx			
9	GWENT COLLEGE	●✦◆	N/A	N/A	BUSINESS & LEGAL STUDIES	S	3	‡					
9	GWENT COLLEGE	●✦◆	N/A	N/A	BUSINESS & ACCOUNTING	S	3	‡					
9	NORTH EAST WALES INSTITUTE	●✦◆	N/A	N/A	COMPUTER STUDIES WITH BUSINESS	S	3			10-4			
9	NORTH EAST WALES INSTITUTE	●✦◆	N/A	N/A	BUSINESS & FINANCE	S	2			8-2	100	65	65
9	SWANSEA UNIVERSITY	●◆	63	86	SPANISH WITH BUSINESS STUDIES	S	4			22-20	53	4	8
9	SWANSEA UNIVERSITY	●◆	63	86	BUSINESS STUDIES WITH YEAR ABROAD	S	4			26-20	353	15	4
9	SWANSEA UNIVERSITY	●◆	63	86	CATALAN & SPANISH WITH BUSINESS STUDIES	S	4			18			
9	SWANSEA UNIVERSITY	●◆	63	86	FRENCH, GERMAN WITH BUSINESS STUDIES	S	4			26-20-24			
9	SWANSEA UNIVERSITY	●◆	63	86	BUSINESS STUDIES	S	3			26-20	648	22	3
9	SWANSEA UNIVERSITY	●◆	63	86	EURO. BUS. ST. (Deferred Choice Of a Mod Lang)	S	4			20			
9	SWANSEA UNIVERSITY	●◆	63	86	LAW AND BUSINESS STUDIES	J	3			BBB			
9	SWANSEA UNIVERSITY	●◆	63	86	CHEMISTRY WITH BUS. STUD. YEAR IN EUROPE	S	4			20	79	9	11
9	SWANSEA UNIVERSITY	●◆	63	86	RUSSIAN,WELSH WITH BUSINESS STUDIES	S	3/4			18			
9	SWANSEA UNIVERSITY	●◆	63	86	CHEMISTRY WITH BUSINESS STUDIES	S	3			18	312	44	14

9	SWANSEA UNIVERSITY	◆◆	63	86	EUROPEAN BUSINESS STUDIES,FR,GER,ITAL,SP	S	4		26-20			
9	SWANSEA UNIVERSITY	◆◆	63	86	ITALIAN FOR BEGINNERS WITH BUS. STUDIES	S	4		18			
9	UNIV OF WALES, ABERYSTWTH	◆◆	35	86	BUSINESS ADMIN WITH A MODERN LANG	S	4		BCC	79	8	10
9	UNIV OF WALES, ABERYSTWTH	◆◆	35	86	BUSINESS ADMINISTRATION & WELSH	S	3		BCC			
9	UNIV OF WALES, ABERYSTWTH	◆◆	35	86	PHYSICS WITH BUSINESS ADMINISTRATION	S	3		14	7	4	57
9	UNIV OF WALES, ABERYSTWTH	◆◆	35	86	LAW & BUSINESS	S	3		BBB-BBC			
9	UNIV OF WALES, ABERYSTWTH	◆◆	35	86	AGRICULTURE WITH BUSINESS STUDIES	S	3		12	92	17	18
9	UNIV OF WALES, ABERYSTWTH	◇◆	35	86	BIOCHEMISTRY WITH BUSINESS ADMIN.	S	3		16	20	5	25
9	UNIV OF WALES, ABERYSTWTH	◆◆	35	86	BUSINESS ADMINISTRATION	S	3		BCC	342	23	7
10	DUNDEE INSTITUTE	◆◆	N/A	N/A	COMMERCE	S	3/4	‡	DD	50		
10	DUNDEE INSTITUTE	✱◆	N/A	N/A	BUSINESS STUDIES	S	4 ✱	‡	DDD	72		
10	EDINBURGH UNIVERSITY	◆◆	26	50	BUSINESS STUDIES/ECONOMICS	J	4		BBC			
10	EDINBURGH UNIVERSITY	◆◆	26	50	MATHS AND BUSINESS STUDIES	J	4		BBC			
10	EDINBURGH UNIVERSITY	◆◆	26	50	BUSINESS STUDIES & FR,GER,SPAN	J	4	L	BBC			
10	EDINBURGH UNIVERSITY	◆◆	26	50	BUSINESS STUDIES AND ACCOUNTING	J	4		BBC			
10	EDINBURGH UNIVERSITY	◆◆	26	50	ARABIC AND BUSINESS STUDIES	J	4	‡	BBC			
10	EDINBURGH UNIVERSITY	◆◆	26	50	PSYCHOLOGY AND BUSINESS STUDIES	J	4		BBB	NEW		
10	EDINBURGH UNIVERSITY	◆◆	26	50	BUSINESS STUDIES AND MATHS	J	4	+	BBC			
10	EDINBURGH UNIVERSITY	◆◆	26	50	BUSINESS STUDIES AND LAW	J	4		BBB			
10	EDINBURGH UNIVERSITY	◆◆	26	50	ELECTRONICS & BUSINESS STUDIES	J	4	‡	CCC	15	3	20
10	EDINBURGH UNIVERSITY	◆◆	26	50	FRENCH & BUSINESS STUDIES	J	4	‡	BBB			
10	EDINBURGH UNIVERSITY	◆◆	26	50	GER,ITAL,SPAN & BUSINESS STUDIES	J	4		BBB			
10	EDINBURGH UNIVERSITY	◆◆	26	50	LAW & BUSINESS STUDIES	J	4	L	ABB			
10	EDINBURGH UNIVERSITY	◆◆	26	50	BCom (WITH/WITHOUT HONS)	S	3/4		BBC	414	43	10
10	GLASGOW CAL UNIVERSITY	☐◆	63	47	BUSINESS STUDIES - HND	S	2	+	CCD-BC	431	45	10
10	GLASGOW CAL UNIVERSITY	☐◆	63	47	BUS. ADMIN WITH TRAVEL & TOURISM - HND	S	2	‡	C	255	61	24
10	GLASGOW CAL UNIVERSITY	☐◆	63	47	EUROPEAN BUSINESS STUDIES	S	3	+	BCC	NEW		
10	GLASGOW CAL UNIVERSITY	☐◆	63	47	BUSINESS STUDIES	S	4	‡	BCC	1723	104	6

TABLE B – BUSINESS STUDIES COURSES (Continued)

	COLLEGE DETAILS				COURSE DETAILS						ENTRY		
REGION	NAME	TYPE	VALUE ADDED	EMPLOYMENT	SUBJECT	TYPE	DURATION	SANDWICH	SUBJECTS REQ	GRADES REQ	APPLY	GET ON	% GET ON
10	GLASGOW CAL UNIVERSITY	□◆	63	47	BUSINESS & MANUFACTURING/SYSTEMS ENG	S	4	5	‡	CD-DDE			
10	HERIOT-WATT UNIVERSITY	◆◆	22	50	INTERNATIONAL BUSINESS & GERMAN,RUSSIAN	S	4		L	BBC			
10	HERIOT-WATT UNIVERSITY	◆◆	22	50	INTERNATIONAL BUSINESS & FRENCH,SPANISH	S	4		L	BBC			
10	HERIOT-WATT UNIVERSITY	◆◆	22	50	INTERNATIONAL BUSINESS & FRENCH,RUSSIAN	S	4		L	BBC			
10	HERIOT-WATT UNIVERSITY	◆◆	22	50	INTERNATIONAL BUSINESS & GERMAN,SPANISH	S	4		L	BBC			
10	HERIOT-WATT UNIVERSITY	◆◆	22	50	INTERNATIONAL BUSINESS & SPANISH,RUSSIAN	S	4		L	BBC			
10	HERIOT-WATT UNIVERSITY	◆◆	22	50	INDUSTRIAL & BUSINESS STUDIES	S	3/4			CCD			
10	HERIOT-WATT UNIVERSITY	◆◆	22	50	INTERNATIONAL BUSINESS & FRENCH,GERMAN	S	4		L	BBC			
10	NAPIER UNIVERSITY	□◆	55	19	BUSINESS ADMINISTRATION - HND	S	2		‡	CC			
10	NAPIER UNIVERSITY	□◆	55	19	COMMERCE	S	3	4		CCC			
10	NAPIER UNIVERSITY	□◆	55	19	BUSINESS STUDIES	S	3	4*	‡	CCD			
10	PAISLEY UNIVERSITY	□◆	26	55	BUSINESS AND MANAGEMENT	S	3/4	4/5		AA-ABC	864	68	8
10	ROBERT GORDON UNIVERSITY	□◆	87	3	EUR BUSINESS ADMIN. WITH LANGUAGE	S	4		‡	BCC	241	44	18
10	ROBERT GORDON UNIVERSITY	□◆	87	3	BUSINESS STUDIES	S	4		‡	CCC	881	104	12
10	ROBERT GORDON UNIVERSITY	□◆	87	3	BUSINESS ADMINISTRATION	S	3	4	‡	CCC			
10	STIRLING UNIVERSITY	◆◆	31	41	BUSINESS STUDIES (&17 COMB OPT) 12	S	4						
10	STIRLING UNIVERSITY	◆◆	31	41	BUSINESS STUDIES	S	4			BBC	904	53	6
10	STIRLING UNIVERSITY	◆◆	31	41	BUSINESS & MANAGEMENT	S	4			BBC	231	9	4
10	STIRLING UNIVERSITY	◆◆	31	41	ACCOUNTANCY/BUSINESS STUDIES (BAcc)	S	4			BBC			
10	STRATHCLYDE UNIVERSITY	◆◆	88	41	TECH & BUSINESS STUDIES (BSc HONS&PASS)	S	3/4		+	CCC			
10	STRATHCLYDE UNIVERSITY	◆◆	68	41	INTERNATIONAL BUSINESS & MOD LANG	S	4		L	BBC			

TABLE C - ECONOMICS COURSES

COLLEGE DETAILS					COURSE DETAILS						ENTRY		
REGION	NAME	TYPE	VALUE ADDED	EMPLOYMENT	SUBJECT	TYPE	DURATION	SANDWICH	SUBJECTS REQ	GRADES REQ	APPLY		% GET ON
1	BRUNEL UNIVERSITY	●★	55	14	BUSINESS ECONOMICS	S	4			BBC	NEW		
1	BRUNEL UNIVERSITY	●◆	55	14	COMPUTING WITH ECONOMICS	S	3			BCC			
1	BRUNEL UNIVERSITY	●★	55	14	COMPUTING WITH ECONOMICS	S	4			BCC	43	5	12
1	BRUNEL UNIVERSITY	●◆	55	14	ECONOMICS	S	4			BBC	126	21	17
1	BRUNEL UNIVERSITY	●◆	55	14	ECONOMICS & BUSINESS FINANCE	J	4			BBC			
1	BRUNEL UNIVERSITY	●◆	55	14	ECONOMICS & MANAGEMENT	J	4			BBC			
1	CITY UNIVERSITY	●◆	4	41	BSc MATHEMATICAL SCIENCE WITH FIN & ECON	S	3	+		14			
1	CITY UNIVERSITY	●◆	4	41	ECONOMICS	S	3			BCC	445	15	3
1	CITY UNIVERSITY	●◆	4	41	ECONOMICS/ACCOUNTING	S	3			BCC			
1	CITY UNIVERSITY	●◆	4	41	ECONOMICS/COMPUTING	S	3			BCC			
1	CITY UNIVERSITY	●◆	4	41	ECONOMICS/PHILOSOPHY	S	3			BCC			
1	CITY UNIVERSITY	●◆	4	41	ECONOMICS/PSYCHOLOGY	S	3			BCC			
1	CITY UNIVERSITY	●◆	4	41	ECONOMICS/SOCIOLOGY	S	3			BCC			
1	CITY UNIVERSITY	●◆	4	41	JOURNALISM/ECONOMICS	J	3			24-18			
1	CITY UNIVERSITY	●◆	4	41	PHILOSOPHY/ECONOMICS	S	3			18			
1	CITY UNIVERSITY	●◆	4	41	PSYCHOLOGY/ECONOMICS	S	3			18			
1	CITY UNIVERSITY	●◆	4	41	SOCIOLOGY/ECONOMICS	S	3			18			
1	EAST LONDON UNIVERSITY	□◆	45	95	APPLIED ECONOMICS	S	3	‡		CC	43	12	28
1	EAST LONDON UNIVERSITY	□◆	45	95	BUSINESS ECONOMICS	S	3	‡		CC	94	11	12
1	EAST LONDON UNIVERSITY	□◆	45	95	ECONOMICS	S	3	‡		CC	153	27	18
1	EAST LONDON UNIVERSITY	□◆	45	95	ECONOMICS &(38 OPT) MJ/MN22	J	3	‡		CC			

				University	Course				Offer			
1	□◆	79	84	GREENWICH UNIVERSITY	ECONOMICS & PSYCHOLOGY	S	3	‡	10	NEW		
1	□◆	79	84	GREENWICH UNIVERSITY	SOCIOLOGY WITH ECONOMICS (MULTI CRSE)	S	3	‡	10	NEW		
1	□◆	79	84	GREENWICH UNIVERSITY	SOCIOLOGY & ECONOMICS (MULTI CRSE)	S	3	‡	10	NEW		
1	□◆	55	79	GUILDHALL UNIVERSITY	ECONOMICS	S	3		CC	503	43	9
1	□◆	55	79	GUILDHALL UNIVERSITY	FINANCIAL ECONOMICS	S	3		CC	197	22	11
1	□◆	55	79	GUILDHALL UNIVERSITY	LEGAL & ECONOMIC STUDIES	S	3	L	CCD			
1	●◆	69	28	KINGSTON UNIVERSITY	APPLIED PHYSICS & ECONOMICS	J	3		8			
1	●◆	69	28	KINGSTON UNIVERSITY	BUSINESS ECONOMICS	S	3	‡	14	NEW		
1	●◆	69	28	KINGSTON UNIVERSITY	ECONOMICS	S	3	‡	14	671	87	13
1	●◆	69	28	KINGSTON UNIVERSITY	ECONOMICS & STATISTICS	J	3		8	NEW		
1	●◆	69	28	KINGSTON UNIVERSITY	FINANCIAL ECONOMICS	S	3	‡	14	NEW		
1	●◆	69	28	KINGSTON UNIVERSITY	GEOGRAPHY & ECONOMICS	J	3		12			
1	●◆	69	28	KINGSTON UNIVERSITY	GEOLOGY & ECONOMICS	J	3		10			
1	●◆	69	28	KINGSTON UNIVERSITY	MATHS & ECONOMICS	J	3		8			
1	✳◆	22	90	LONDON SCHOOL OF ECONOMICS	ECONOMETRICS & MATHEMATICAL ECONOMICS	S	3	+	24	46	9	20
1	✳◆	22	90	LONDON SCHOOL OF ECONOMICS	ECONOMICS	S	3		24	1		
1	✳◆	22	90	LONDON SCHOOL OF ECONOMICS	ECONOMICS & ECONOMIC HISTORY	S	3		24	99	9	9
1	✳◆	22	90	LONDON SCHOOL OF ECONOMICS	MATHS & ECONOMICS	S	3		24	79	9	11
1	✳◆	22	90	LONDON SCHOOL OF ECONOMICS	PHILOSOPHY & ECONOMICS	S	3		24	117	7	6
1	●◆	91	3	MIDDLESEX UNIVERSITY	ECONOMICS	S	4		14-12			
1	●◆	91	3	MIDDLESEX UNIVERSITY	EUROPEAN ECONOMICS -FRENCH,SPANISH	J	4	+&L	12-8			
1	✳◆	79	55	Q.M. & W. COLL - UNIV. OF LONDON	BUSINESS ECONOMICS	S	3	+	BCC			
1	✳◆	79	55	Q.M. & W. COLL - UNIV. OF LONDON	ECONOMICS	S	3		BCC			
1	✳◆	79	55	Q.M. & W. COLL - UNIV. OF LONDON	ECONOMICS (& 9 COMB OPT) 20	S	3/4					
1	●◆	79	55	Q.M. & W. COLL - UNIV. OF LONDON	GEOGRAPHY & BUSINESS ECONOMICS	S	3		BCC			
1	✳◆	79	55	Q.M. & W. COLL - UNIV. OF LONDON	MATHEMATICS & BUSINESS ECONOMICS	S	3	+	BCC			
1	✳◆	79	55	Q.M. & W. COLL - UNIV. OF LONDON	STATISTICS/MATHEMATICS & BUSINESS ECONS	S	3	+	BCC			
1	✳◆	35	34	ROYAL HOLLOWAY - U OF LONDON	ECONOMICS & MANAGEMENT STUDIES	S	3		BBC			

TABLE C - ECONOMICS COURSES (Continued)

	COLLEGE DETAILS					COURSE DETAILS					ENTRY		
REGION	NAME	TYPE	VALUE ADDED	EMPLOYMENT	SUBJECT	TYPE	DURATION	SANDWICH	SUBJECTS REQ	GRADES REQ	APPLY	% GET ON	
1	ROYAL HOLLOWAY - U OF LONDON	✳❖	35	34	ECONOMICS & PUBLIC ADMINISTRATION	S	3			BCC			
1	ROYAL HOLLOWAY - U OF LONDON	❖	35	34	ECONOMICS & SOCIAL POLICY	S	3			BCC			
1	ROYAL HOLLOWAY - U OF LONDON	✳❖	35	34	ECONOMICS(& 28 MJ/MN OPT)21	J	3/4						
1	ROYAL HOLLOWAY - U OF LONDON	✳	35	34	SOCIOLOGY & ECONOMICS	S	3			BCC			
1	SOAS - UNIVERSITY OF LONDON	✳❖	N/A	N/A	DEVELOPMENT STUDIES & ECONOMICS	S	3			BBC			
1	SOAS - UNIVERSITY OF LONDON	✳	N/A	N/A	ECONOMICS	S	3			BB-BCC	122	15	12
1	SOAS - UNIVERSITY OF LONDON	✳❖	N/A	N/A	ECONOMICS WITH ASIAN/AFRICAN LANGUAGE	S	3/4			BB-BCC	14	2	14
1	SOAS - UNIVERSITY OF LONDON	✳❖	N/A	N/A	ECONOMICS & GEOGRAPHY	S	3			BB-BCC			
1	SOAS - UNIVERSITY OF LONDON	✳❖	N/A	N/A	ECONOMICS & HISTORY	S	3			BB-BCC			
1	SOAS - UNIVERSITY OF LONDON	✳❖	N/A	N/A	ECONOMICS & LAW	S	3			AB-BBB			
1	SOAS - UNIVERSITY OF LONDON	✳❖	N/A	N/A	ECONOMICS & POLITICS	S	3			BB-BCC			
1	SOAS - UNIVERSITY OF LONDON	✳❖	N/A	N/A	ECONOMICS & RELIGEOUS STUDIES	S	3			BB-BCC			
1	SOAS - UNIVERSITY OF LONDON	✳❖	N/A	N/A	ECONOMICS & SOCIAL ANTHROPOLOGY	S	3			BBC			
1	THAMES VALLEY UNIVERSITY	●❖	63	24	BUSINESS ECONOMICS	S	3			8			
1	THAMES VALLEY UNIVERSITY	●❖	63	24	ECONOMICS	S	3			8	128	56	44
1	THAMES VALLEY UNIVERSITY	●❖	63	24	ECONOMICS WITH FRENCH,GERMAN,SPANISH	S	3			8			
1	UNIVERSITY COLL. - U OF LONDON	✳❖	41	93	AGRICULTURAL ECONOMICS	S	3			16	43	8	19
1	UNIVERSITY COLL. - U OF LONDON	✳❖	41	93	ECONOMICS	S	3	‡		BBC	757	81	11
1	UNIVERSITY COLL. - U OF LONDON	✳❖	93	93	ECONOMICS & GEOGRAPHY	S	3	‡		BCC			
1	UNIVERSITY COLL. - U OF LONDON	✳❖	93	93	ECONOMICS & HISTORY	S	3	‡		BBC			
1	UNIVERSITY COLL. - U OF LONDON	✳❖	41	93	ECONOMICS & STATISTICS	S	3	+		▶			

	UNIVERSITY / COLLEGE OF LONDON					S			+/£	CC			
1	WESTMINSTER UNIVERSITY	□◆	91	10	ECONOMICS FOR BUSINESS	S	3			CC			
2	KENT UNIVERSITY	◆◆	47	74	ACCOUNTING/ECONOMICS	J	3			20			
2	KENT UNIVERSITY	◆◆	47	74	COMPUTING/ECONOMICS	J	3			BCC			
2	KENT UNIVERSITY	◆◆	47	74	DEVELOPMENT STUDIES (ECONOMICS)	S	3			BCC			
2	KENT UNIVERSITY	◆◆	47	74	ECONOMICS	S	3			BCC	426	22	5
2	KENT UNIVERSITY	◆◆	47	74	ECONOMICS WITH A LANGUAGE	S	3		L	20	15		
2	KENT UNIVERSITY	◆◆	47	74	ECONOMICS WITH COMPUTING	S	3			BCC	39	2	5
2	KENT UNIVERSITY	◆◆	47	74	ECONOMICS WITH ECONOMETRICS	S	3		+	20	27	2	7
2	KENT UNIVERSITY	◆◆	47	74	ECONOMICS & PHYSICS	S	3		‡	20			
2	KENT UNIVERSITY	◆◆	47	74	ECONOMICS (& 5 COMB OPT) 35	J	3						
2	KENT UNIVERSITY	◆◆	47	74	EUROPEAN ECONOMICS (FRENCH)	S	4		L	BCC	62	4	6
2	KENT UNIVERSITY	◆◆	47	74	EUROPEAN ECONOMICS (GERMAN)	S	4		L	BCC	25	2	8
2	KENT UNIVERSITY	◆◆	47	74	EUROPEAN ECONOMICS (SPANISH)	S	4		L	BCC	23	1	4
2	KENT UNIVERSITY	◆◆	47	74	EUROPEAN STUDIES (ECONOMICS)	S	4		‡	BCC			
2	KENT UNIVERSITY	◆◆	47	74	INDUSTRIAL RELATIONS (ECONOMICS)	S	3			BCC			
2	KENT UNIVERSITY	◆◆	47	74	MATHEMATICS & ECONOMICS	S	3/4		+	20			
2	KENT UNIVERSITY	◆◆	47	74	URBAN STUDIES (ECONOMICS)	S	3			BCC			
2	PORTSMOUTH UNIVERSITY	□◆	61	14	ACCOUNTING & ECONOMICS	S	3	4		14	NEW		
2	PORTSMOUTH UNIVERSITY	□◆	61	14	ECONOMICS	S	3			14	823	115	14
2	PORTSMOUTH UNIVERSITY	□◆	61	14	ECONOMICS & GEOGRAPHY	S	3			14			
2	READING UNIVERSITY	◆◆	85	55	AGRICULTURAL ECONOMICS	S	3		‡	CCD-BB	104	32	31
2	READING UNIVERSITY	◆◆	85	55	BUSINESS ECONOMICS	S	3			BBC	656	8	1
2	READING UNIVERSITY	◆◆	85	55	BUSINESS ECONS & ORGANISATIONAL STUDIES	S	3			BCC			
2	READING UNIVERSITY	◆◆	85	55	ECONOMICS	S	3			BBC	530	25	5
2	READING UNIVERSITY	◆◆	85	55	ECONOMICS (& 12 OPT) BA HONS 36	S	3/4						
2	READING UNIVERSITY	◆◆	85	55	REGIONAL SCIENCE(GEOGRAPHY & ECON.)	S	3			BCC			
2	SOUTHAMPTON UNIVERSITY	◆◆	35	74	ACCOUNTING & ECONOMICS	J	3			22			
2	SOUTHAMPTON UNIVERSITY	◆◆	35	74	ECONOMICS	S	3			22	383	34	

TABLE C - ECONOMICS COURSES (Continued)

	COLLEGE DETAILS				COURSE DETAILS						ENTRY		
REGION	NAME	TYPE	VALUE ADDED	EMPLOYMENT	SUBJECT	TYPE	DURATION	SANDWICH	SUBJECTS REQ	GRADES REQ	APPLY	GET ON	%
2	SOUTHAMPTON UNIVERSITY	◆◆	35	74	ECONOMICS WITH ACTUARIAL STUDIES	S		+		22	32	9	28
2	SOUTHAMPTON UNIVERSITY	◆◆	35	74	ECONOMICS & BUSINESS ECONOMICS	J	3			22			
2	SOUTHAMPTON UNIVERSITY	◆◆	35	74	ECONOMICS & ECONOMIC HISTORY	J	3			22			
2	SOUTHAMPTON UNIVERSITY	◆◆	35	74	ECONOMICS & FRENCH, GERMAN	J	4			22			
2	SOUTHAMPTON UNIVERSITY	◆◆	35	74	ECONOMICS & MATHS	J	3			22			
2	SOUTHAMPTON UNIVERSITY	◆◆	35	74	ECONOMICS & PHILOSOPHY	J	3			22			
2	SOUTHAMPTON UNIVERSITY	◆◆	35	74	ECONOMICS & QUANTITATIVE ECONOMICS	J	3	+		22	11	1	9
2	SOUTHAMPTON UNIVERSITY	◆◆	35	74	ECONOMICS & SOCIOLOGY	J	3			22			
2	SOUTHAMPTON UNIVERSITY	◆◆	35	74	ECONOMICS & STATISTICS	J	3	+		22	37	2	5
2	SOUTHAMPTON UNIVERSITY	◆◆	35	74	MATHS WITH ECONOMICS	S	3	+		BCC	49	7	14
2	SURREY UNIVERSITY	◆◆	4	3	BUSINESS ECONOMICS WITH COMPUTING	S	3	4		22	263	30	11
2	SURREY UNIVERSITY	◆◆	4	3	ECONOMICS	S	3	4		22	243	39	16
2	SURREY UNIVERSITY	◆◆	4	3	ECONOMICS & SOCIOLOGY	S	3	4		20			
2	SURREY UNIVERSITY	◆◆	4	3	GERMAN,FRENCH & ECON WITH INTL BUS	S	4	L		BCC-BBC			
2	SURREY UNIVERSITY	◆◆	4	3	RUSSIAN & ECONOMICS WITH INTL BUSINESS	S	4	‡		BBC			
2	SUSSEX UNIVERSITY	◆◆	22	84	ECONOMICS IN AFRICAN/ASIAN STUDIES	S	3			BCC	36	7	19
2	SUSSEX UNIVERSITY	◆◆	22	84	ECONOMICS IN EUROPEAN STUDIES	S	4	‡		BCC	107	14	13
2	SUSSEX UNIVERSITY	◆◆	22	84	ECONOMICS IN SOCIAL SCIENCE	S	3			BCC	155	20	13
2	SUSSEX UNIVERSITY	◆◆	22	84	ECONOMICS WITH DEVELOPMENT STUDIES	S	3			BCC	66	10	15
2	SUSSEX UNIVERSITY	◆◆	22	84	ECONOMICS WITH ECONOMIC HISTORY	S	3			BCC	73	7	10
2	SUSSEX UNIVERSITY	◆◆	22	84	ECONOMICS WITH FRENCH/MAITRISE INTL	S	4	‡		BCC			

				University	Course	S/J	No.		Offer			
2				SUSSEX UNIVERSITY	(…AL & ECONOMICS)	S			BCC			
2	♦♦	22	84	SUSSEX UNIVERSITY	MATHEMATICS & STATISTICS WITH ECONOMICS	S			BCC			
2	♦♦	22	84	SUSSEX UNIVERSITY	MATHS WITH ECONOMICS	S	3	‡	BCC	317	56	18
2	♦♦	22	84	SUSSEX UNIVERSITY	MATHS & ECONOMICS	S	3	+	BCC			
3	♦♦	26	24	BATH UNIVERSITY	ECONOMICS	S	3		22	298	33	11
3	♦♦	26	24	BATH UNIVERSITY	ECONOMICS WITH COMPUTING & STATISTICS	S	4		22	24		
3	♦♦	26	24	BATH UNIVERSITY	ECONOMICS WITH COMPUTING & STATISTICS	S	3		22	25	3	
3	♦♦	26	24	BATH UNIVERSITY	ECONOMICS & POLITICS	J	3/4		22			
3	♦♦	26	24	BATH UNIVERSITY	ECONOMICS	S	4		22	113	14	12
3	♦♦	35	30	BRISTOL UNIV (UWE)	ECONOMICS	S	3		14			
3	♦♦	14	67	BRISTOL UNIVERSITY	ECON WITH STATS & STUDY IN EUROPE	S	4	+	ABB	NEW		
3	♦♦	14	67	BRISTOL UNIVERSITY	ECONOMICS	S	3	+	ABB(S)	294	40	14
3	♦♦	14	67	BRISTOL UNIVERSITY	ECONOMICS WITH STATISTICS	S	3	+	ABB	35	7	20
3	♦♦	14	67	BRISTOL UNIVERSITY	ECONOMICS WITH STUDY IN EUROPE	S	4	+	ABB	NEW		
3	♦♦	14	67	BRISTOL UNIVERSITY	ECONOMICS & ACC WITH STUDY IN EUR	S	4	+/L	ABC-BBC			
3	♦♦	14	67	BRISTOL UNIVERSITY	ECONOMICS & ACCOUNTING	S	3	+/L	ABC-BBC			
3	♦♦	14	67	BRISTOL UNIVERSITY	ECONOMICS & ECONOMIC HISTORY	S	3		ABC-BBC			
3	♦♦	14	67	BRISTOL UNIVERSITY	ECONOMICS & MATHS	S	3	+/L	ABC(S)			
3	♦♦	14	67	BRISTOL UNIVERSITY	ECONOMICS & POLITICS	S	3		ABB			
3	♦♦	14	67	BRISTOL UNIVERSITY	ECONOMICS & SOCIOLOGY	S	3		ABC			
3	♦♦	14	67	BRISTOL UNIVERSITY	PHILOSOPHY & ECONOMICS	J	3		ABB-ABC			
3	♦♦	1	62	EXETER UNIVERSITY	BUSINESS ECONOMICS	S	3		ABB	1		
3	♦♦	1	62	EXETER UNIVERSITY	BUSINESS ECON. WITH EUROPEAN STUDY	S	4	L	ABB			
3	♦♦	1	62	EXETER UNIVERSITY	EC OF AGRIC,FOOD & NAT RES W/EURO STUDY	S	4	L	BBC	4	1	25
3	♦♦	1	62	EXETER UNIVERSITY	ECON OF AGRIC,FOOD & NAT RES	S	3		BBC	49	17	
3	♦♦	1	62	EXETER UNIVERSITY	ECONOMICS	S	3		ABB	481	50	10
3	♦♦	1	62	EXETER UNIVERSITY	ECONOMICS WITH EUROPEAN STUD	S	4	L	ABB	97	6	6
3	♦♦	1	62	EXETER UNIVERSITY	ECONOMICS & GEOGRAPHY	J	3		BBB			
3	♦♦	1	62	EXETER UNIVERSITY	ECONOMICS & GEOGRAPHY WITH EURO STUDY	J	4	L	BBB			

TABLE C - ECONOMICS COURSES (Continued)

REGION	COLLEGE DETAILS				COURSE DETAILS						ENTRY	
	NAME	TYPE	VALUE ADDED	EMPLOYMENT	SUBJECT	TYPE	DURATION	SANDWICH	SUBJECTS REQ	GRADES REQ	APPLY	GET ON %
3	EXETER UNIVERSITY	◆◆	1	62	ECONOMICS & POLITICS	S	3			ABB		
3	EXETER UNIVERSITY	◆◆	1	62	ECON. & POLITICS WITH EUROPEAN STUDY	S	4	L		ABB		
3	EXETER UNIVERSITY	◆◆	1	62	ECONOMICS & STATISTICS	S	4	+		BBC	72	14 · 19
3	EXETER UNIVERSITY	◆◆	1	62	ECON. & STATISTICS WITH EUROPEAN STUDY	S	4	+ & L		BBC	14	2 · 14
3	PLYMOUTH UNIVERSITY	□◆	55	34	ECONOMICS (APP)	S	3			CCD-BC		
3	PLYMOUTH UNIVERSITY	□◆	55	34	ECONOMICS(APP) & 17 OPT 38	S	3	‡		▶		
3	PLYMOUTH UNIVERSITY	□◆	55	34	INTERNATIONAL RELATIONS WITH ECONOMICS	S	3	‡		▶		
3	PLYMOUTH UNIVERSITY	□◆	55	34	STATISTICS (APP) WITH ECONOMICS (APP)	S	3	‡		▶		
3	PLYMOUTH UNIVERSITY	□◆	55	34	STATS (APP) WITH MGT SC WITH ECON (APP)	S	3	‡		▶		
4	BIRMINGHAM UNIVERSITY	◆◆	85	67	ECONOMICS	S	3			BBC	709	29 · 4
4	BIRMINGHAM UNIVERSITY	◆◆	85	67	ECONOMICS WITH FRENCH	S	4	‡		BBC	77	3 · 4
4	BIRMINGHAM UNIVERSITY	◆◆	85	67	ECONOMICS WITH GERMAN	S	4	‡		BBC	25	2 · 8
4	BIRMINGHAM UNIVERSITY	◆◆	85	67	ECONOMICS WITH SPANISH	J	3	‡		BBC		
4	BIRMINGHAM UNIVERSITY	◆◆	85	67	ECONOMICS & GEOGRAPHY	S	4	‡		BBC	20	2 · 10
4	BIRMINGHAM UNIVERSITY	◆◆	85	67	ECONOMICS & MODERN ECONOMIC HISTORY	S	3			BBC		
4	BIRMINGHAM UNIVERSITY	◆◆	85	67	ECONOMICS & POLITICAL SCIENCE	J	3			BBC		
4	BIRMINGHAM UNIVERSITY	◆◆	85	67	ECONOMICS & STATISTICS	S	3	+		BBC		
4	BIRMINGHAM UNIVERSITY	◆◆	85	67	INTERNATIONAL STUDIES WITH ECONOMICS	S	3			BBC		
4	BIRMINGHAM UNIVERSITY	◆◆	85	67	MATHEMATICAL ECONOMICS	S	3	+		BBC	56	6
4	BIRMINGHAM UNIVERSITY	◆◆	85	67	PLANNING & ECONOMICS	J	3			BBC		
4	BUCKINGHAM UNIVERSITY	◆◆	46	1	ACCOUNTING WITH ECONOMICS	S	2			18	17	

				Course								
4	●◆	46	1	COMPUTER SCIENCE WITH ECONOMICS	S	2			16			
4	●◆	46	1	ECONOMICS	S	2		+/£	16	56	4	7
4	●◆	46	1	ECONOMICS WITH FR, GER, SPAN	S	2			12	7	1	
4	●◆	46	1	POLITICS & ECONOMICS	S	2			12			
4	●◆	53	14	ECONOMICS	S	3			14	714	104	15
4	●◆	53	14	ECONOMICS WITH ACCOUNTING	S	3			14			
4	●◆	53	14	ECONOMICS WITH EUROPEAN STUDIES	S	3			14			
4	●◆	53	14	ECONOMICS WITH GOVERNMENT	S	3			14			
4	●◆	53	14	ECONOMICS WITH LAW	S	3			14			
4	●◆	53	14	ECONOMICS WITH MANAGEMENT	S	3			14			
4	●◆	53	14	ECONOMICS WITH MARKETING	S	3			14			
4	□◆	47	18	BIOLOGY & ECONOMICS	S		4		10			
4	□◆	47	18	COMPUTER SCIENCE & ECONOMICS	S	4			16-12			
4	□◆	47	18	ECONOMICS & FRENCH	S	3			14			
4	□◆	47	18	ECONOMICS & GEOGRAPHY	S	3			16-14			
4	□◆	47	18	ECONOMICS & GERMAN	S	3		‡	14			
4	□◆	47	16	ECONOMICS & MATHEMATICS	S		4		18			
4	□◆	47	18	ECONOMICS & STATISTICS	S		4		16-14			
4	□◆	47	18	ECONOMICS (FINANCIAL OR INDUSTRIAL)	S	3			16-14	850	80	9
4	□◆	79	2	ECONOMICS	S	3			14	963	75	8
4	●◆	4	67	ECONOMICS & 3 DBL LANG COMB 23	J	3/4		‡	BBC			
4	●◆	4	67	ECONOMICS (& 6 OPT) SOC SCS 23	J	3/4		‡				
4	●◆	4	67	ECONOMICS& 26 OPT MULTIGPS 23	J	3/4		‡				
4	●◆	15	74	BUSINESS ECONOMICS (BA HONS)	S	3			BBC	601	34	6
4	●◆	15	74	BUSINESS ECONOMICS (BSc (ECON) HONS)	S	3		*	BBC	174	11	6
4	●◆	15	74	ECONOMICS & ECONOMIC HISTORY	J	3			BCC			
4	●◆	15	74	ECONOMICS & LAW	J	3			BBB			
4	●◆	15	74	ECONOMICS (BA HONS)	S	3			BBC	377	41	11
4	●◆	15	74	ECONOMICS (BSc (ECON) HONS)	S	3		*	BBC	99	18	18

| | COLLEGE DETAILS | | | | COURSE DETAILS | | | | | ENTRY | | |
REGION	NAME	TYPE	VALUE ADDED	EMPLOYMENT	SUBJECT	TYPE	DURATION	SANDWICH / SUBJECTS REQ	GRADES REQ	APPLY	GET ON	%
4	LOUGHBOROUGH UNIVERSITY	●◆	41	34	ECONOMICS	S	3		BBC	481	51	11
4	LOUGHBOROUGH UNIVERSITY	●◆	41	34	ECONOMICS WITH ACCOUNTING	S	3		BBC	233	23	10
4	LOUGHBOROUGH UNIVERSITY	●◆	41	34	ECONOMICS WITH MINOR SUBJ	S	3		BBC	235	33	14
4	LOUGHBOROUGH UNIVERSITY	●◆	41	34	HUMAN GEOGRAPHY & ECONOMICS	S	3		BCC			
4	LOUGHBOROUGH UNIVERSITY	●◆	41	34	MATHEMATICS WITH ECONOMICS	S	3		BCC	84	14	17
4	NENE COLLEGE	●◆	N/A	N/A	COMBINED STUDIES WITH ECONOMICS	J	3		8 Approx	100	60	60
4	NENE COLLEGE	●◆	N/A	N/A	ECONOMICS	S		‡				
4	NOTTINGHAM TRENT UNIVERSITY	●◆	31	14	BUSINESS ECONOMICS	S	3	‡	18	2	5	250
4	NOTTINGHAM TRENT UNIVERSITY	●◆	31	14	ECONOMICS	S	3	‡	18	1670	101	6
4	NOTTINGHAM TRENT UNIVERSITY	●◆	31	14	EUROPEAN ECONOMICS WITH DUTCH	S	4	‡	16	26	11	42
4	NOTTINGHAM TRENT UNIVERSITY	●◆	31	14	EUROPEAN ECONOMICS WITH FRENCH	S	4	‡	16	8	8	100
4	NOTTINGHAM TRENT UNIVERSITY	●◆	31	14	EUROPEAN ECONOMICS WITH GERMAN	S	4	‡	16	19	3	16
4	NOTTINGHAM TRENT UNIVERSITY	●◆	31	14	EUROPEAN ECONOMICS WITH ITALIAN	S	4	‡	16			
4	NOTTINGHAM TRENT UNIVERSITY	●◆	31	14	EUROPEAN ECONOMICS WITH SPANISH	S	4	‡	16	2	2	
4	NOTTINGHAM UNIVERSITY	●◆	86	28	ECONOMICS	S	3		ABB	811	54	7
4	NOTTINGHAM UNIVERSITY	●◆	86	28	ECONOMICS & AGRICULTURAL ECONOMICS	J	3		ABB	30	2	7
4	NOTTINGHAM UNIVERSITY	●◆	86	28	ECONOMICS & ECONOMETRICS	S	3	+	ABB	66	11	17
4	NOTTINGHAM UNIVERSITY	●◆	86	28	ECONOMICS & PHILOSOPHY	J	3		ABB		2	
4	NOTTINGHAM UNIVERSITY	●◆	86	28	INDUSTRIAL ECONOMICS	S	3		BBB	196	21	11
4	NOTTINGHAM UNIVERSITY	●◆	86	28	INDUSTRIAL ECONOMICS WITH ACCOUNTING	S	3		BBB			
4	NOTTINGHAM UNIVERSITY	●◆	86	28	INDUSTRIAL ECONOMICS WITH INSURANCE	S	3		BBB	41	1	2

	University		31	12	Economics (& 39 Comb Opt) 37	S	3/4	CCD-BB			
4	OXFORD BROOKES UNIVERSITY	□◇	31	12	ECONOMICS (& 39 COMB OPT) 37	S	3/4	CCD-BB			
4	OXFORD UNIVERSITY	●◇	10	10	ECONOMICS & MANAGEMENT	S	3	AAB-ABB			
4	OXFORD UNIVERSITY	●◆	10	10	ENGINEERING & ECONOMICS	S	4 ‡	AAB			
4	OXFORD UNIVERSITY	●◇	10	10	MODERN HISTORY & ECONOMICS	S	3 ‡	AAB-ABB			
4	OXFORD UNIVERSITY	●◇	10	10	PHILOSOPHY, POLITICS & ECONOMICS	S					
4	STAFFORDSHIRE UNIVERSITY	●◇	63	47	APPLIED STATISTICS & ECONOMICS	J	3 ‡	CC-DD			
4	STAFFORDSHIRE UNIVERSITY	●◇	63	47	BUSINESS & FINANCIAL ECONOMICS	S	3	CC			
4	STAFFORDSHIRE UNIVERSITY	●◇	63	47	COMPUTING & ECONOMICS	J	3	CC			
4	STAFFORDSHIRE UNIVERSITY	●◇	63	47	ECONOMICS	S	3	CC			
4	STAFFORDSHIRE UNIVERSITY	●◇	63	47	ECONOMICS & GEOGRAPHY	J	3	BC-BCC			
4	STAFFORDSHIRE UNIVERSITY	●◇	63	47	EUROPEAN ECONOMICS	S	3	CC			
4	STAFFORDSHIRE UNIVERSITY	●◇	63	47	FR,GER,SPAN & EUR ECONOMICS	J	3	4	BC-BCC			
4	WARWICK UNIVERSITY	●◇	19	55	ECONOMICS	S	3	ABC-BBB	650	60	9
4	WARWICK UNIVERSITY	●◇	19	55	ECONOMICS & ECONOMIC HISTORY	S	3	ABC-BBB			
4	WARWICK UNIVERSITY	●◇	19	55	ECONOMICS & INTERNATIONAL STUDIES	S	3	ABC-BBB			
4	WARWICK UNIVERSITY	●◇	19	55	ECONOMICS & POLITICS	S	3	ABC-BBB			
4	WARWICK UNIVERSITY	●◇	19	55	INDUSTRIAL ECONOMICS	S	3	ABC-BBB	110	8	7
4	WARWICK UNIVERSITY	●◇	19	55	ITALIAN WITH ECONOMICS	S	4	BBB	9		
4	WARWICK UNIVERSITY	●◇	19	55	MATHEMATICS & ECONOMICS	S	3	4 +	ABB			
4	WOLVERHAMPTON UNIVERSITY	●◇	91	50	BUSINESS ECONOMICS	S	3 ‡	▶			
4	WOLVERHAMPTON UNIVERSITY	●◇	91	50	ECONOMICS	S	3 ‡	14			
5	ANGLIA POLY UNIV	●◇	53	8	BUS ECONOMICS(&13 MOD OPT) 34	J	3				
5	ANGLIA POLY UNIV	●◆	53	8	BUSINESS ECONOMICS	S	3	12	105	39	37
5	ANGLIA POLY UNIV	●◆	53	8	EUROPEAN BUSINESS ECONOMICS	S	4	12			
5	ANGLIA POLY UNIV	●◆	53	8	FR,GER,IT,SPAN/BUS ECONOMICS	J	4	14			
5	CAMBRIDGE UNIVERSITY	●◇	2	34	ECONOMICS	S	3	ABB-AAA	568	150	26
5	EAST ANGLIA UNIVERSITY	●◇	13	79	BUSINESS FINANCE & ECONOMICS	S	3	BBB-BBC			
5	EAST ANGLIA UNIVERSITY	●◇	13	79	ECONOMICS	S	3	BBC	193	39	20
5	EAST ANGLIA UNIVERSITY	●◇	13	79	ECONOMICS WITH MODERN EUROPEAN LANG	S	3 ‡	BCC			

TABLE C – ECONOMICS COURSES (Continued)

| | COLLEGE DETAILS | | | | COURSE DETAILS | | | | | | ENTRY | |
| | | | VALUE ADDED | EMPLOYMENT | | | | | | | APPLY | GET ON % |
REGION	NAME	TYPE			SUBJECT	TYPE	DURATION	SANDWICH	SUBJECTS REQ	GRADES REQ		
5	EAST ANGLIA UNIVERSITY	◆◆	13	79	ECONOMICS WITH ACCOUNTING	S	3	‡		BBC	102	7	7
5	EAST ANGLIA UNIVERSITY	◆◆	13	79	ECONOMICS & ECONOMIC & SOCIAL HISTORY	S	3			BBC			
5	EAST ANGLIA UNIVERSITY	◆◆	13	79	ECONOMICS & PHILOSOPHY	S	3	‡		BCC			
5	EAST ANGLIA UNIVERSITY	◆◆	13	79	MATHS WITH ECONOMICS	S	3			BCC	26	7	27
5	EAST ANGLIA UNIVERSITY	◆◆	13	79	POLITICS & ECONOMICS	S	3			BBC			
5	EAST ANGLIA UNIVERSITY	◆◆	13	79	SOCIOLOGY & ECONOMICS	S	3			BBC			
5	ESSEX UNIVERSITY	◆◆	10	79	ACCOUNTING, FINANCE & ECONOMICS	J	3	+		BCC			
5	ESSEX UNIVERSITY	◆◆	10	79	ECONOMICS	S	3			BCC	429	52	12
5	ESSEX UNIVERSITY	◆◆	10	79	ECONOMICS & ECONOMETRICS	S	3	+		BCC	8	1	13
5	ESSEX UNIVERSITY	◆◆	10	79	ECONOMICS & ECONOMETRICS	S	3	+		BCC	25		
5	ESSEX UNIVERSITY	◆◆	10	79	ECONOMICS & POLITICS	S	3			BCC			
5	ESSEX UNIVERSITY	◆◆	10	79	HISTORY & ECONOMICS	J	3			BCC			
5	ESSEX UNIVERSITY	◆◆	10	79	MATHS,OPERATIONAL RESEARCH & ECON.	S	3			18	74	9	12
5	HERTFORDSHIRE UNIVERSITY	◆◆	79	3	APPLIED ECONOMICS	S	3	‡		16	279	69	25
5	HULL UNIVERSITY	◆◆	47	62	ECONOMICS	S	3	‡		BBC	245	28	11
5	HULL UNIVERSITY	◆◆	47	62	ECONOMICS & ACCOUNTING	S	3	‡		BBC			
5	HULL UNIVERSITY	◆◆	47	62	ECONOMICS & BUSINESS ECONOMICS	S	3	‡		BBC	251	26	10
5	HULL UNIVERSITY	◆◆	47	62	ECONOMICS & ECONOMIC HISTORY	S	3	‡		BBB-BCC			
5	HULL UNIVERSITY	◆◆	47	62	ECONOMICS/GEOGRAPHY	J	3	‡		BCC(S)			
5	HULL UNIVERSITY	◆◆	47	62	INTERNATIONAL & FINANCIAL ECONOMICS	S	3	‡					
6	BRADFORD UNIVERSITY	◆◆	91	50	ECONOMICS	S	3			CCC-BB	452	39	9

				University	Course							
6	●◆	17	41	DURHAM UNIVERSITY	ECONOMICS	S	3		ABC	265	73	28
6	◆	17	41	DURHAM UNIVERSITY	ECONOMICS WITH FRENCH	S	4	L	ABC			
6	●◆	17	41	DURHAM UNIVERSITY	ECONOMICS & HISTORY	J	3		ABC			
6	●◆	17	41	DURHAM UNIVERSITY	ECONOMICS & LAW	J	3		ABB			
6	●◆	17	41	DURHAM UNIVERSITY	ECONOMICS & POLITICS	J	3		ABC			
6	●◆	17	41	DURHAM UNIVERSITY	ECONOMICS & SOCIOLOGY	J	3		ABC			
6	●◆	17	41	DURHAM UNIVERSITY	MATHS & ECONOMICS	J	4	+	ABC			
6	□◆	91	8	LEEDS METRO UNIVERSITY	ECONOMICS & PUBLIC POLICY	S	3	4	CC Approx.	855	67	8
6	●◆	41	62	LEEDS UNIVERSITY	CHINESE WITH ECONOMICS	S	4		BBC			
6	●●◆	41	62	LEEDS UNIVERSITY	ECONOMIC STUDIES	S	3		BBC	640	62	10
6	●◆	41	62	LEEDS UNIVERSITY	ECONOMICS & JAPANESE STUDIES	S	4		BBC			
6	●◆	41	62	LEEDS UNIVERSITY	ECONOMICS (& 16 OPT) BA HONS 25	S	3/4					
6	●◆	19	34	NEWCASTLE UNIVERSITY	AGRICULTURAL ECONOMICS	S	3		CCC	71	18	25
6	●◆	19	34	NEWCASTLE UNIVERSITY	COMPUTER SCIENCE & ECONOMICS	J	3	+	BCC			
6	●◆	19	34	NEWCASTLE UNIVERSITY	ECONOMICS	S	3	‡	BCC	371	54	15
6	●◆	19	34	NEWCASTLE UNIVERSITY	ECONOMICS & ACCOUNTING	S	3		BBC			
6	●◆	19	34	NEWCASTLE UNIVERSITY	ECONOMICS & BUSINESS MANAGEMENT	S	3	‡	BCC			
6	●◆	19	34	NEWCASTLE UNIVERSITY	ECONOMICS & GEOGRAPHY	S	3		BBC			
6	●◆	19	34	NEWCASTLE UNIVERSITY	ECONOMICS & MATHS	J	3	+	BCC			
6	●◆	19	34	NEWCASTLE UNIVERSITY	ECONOMICS & SOCIAL POLICY	S	3		BCC			
6	●◆	19	34	NEWCASTLE UNIVERSITY	ECONOMICS & STATISTICS	J	3	+	BCC			
6	●◆	19	34	NEWCASTLE UNIVERSITY	FINANCE & BUSINESS ECONOMICS	S	3	‡	BCC			
6	●◆	19	34	NEWCASTLE UNIVERSITY	POLITICS & ECONOMICS	S	3	‡	BCC			
6	□◆	47	88	NORTHUMBRIA UNIVERSITY	ECONOMICS	S	3	‡	16	678	83	12
6	□◆	47	88	NORTHUMBRIA UNIVERSITY	ECONOMICS	S	2	‡	16	10	1	10
6	●◆	10	47	SHEFFIELD UNIVERSITY	ACCOUNTANCY & FINANCIAL MGT/ ECONOMICS	S	3		BBB			
6	●◆	10	47	SHEFFIELD UNIVERSITY	BUSINESS STUDIES/ECONOMICS	S	3		BBB			
6	●◆	10	47	SHEFFIELD UNIVERSITY	ECONOMICS	S	3		BBB	408	47	12

TABLE C - ECONOMICS COURSES (Continued)

REGION	NAME	TYPE	VALUE ADDED	EMPLOYMENT	SUBJECT	TYPE	DURATION	SANDWICH	SUBJECTS REQ	GRADES REQ	APPLY	% GET ON
6	SHEFFIELD UNIVERSITY	◆◆	10	47	ECONOMICS WITH ECONOMETRICS	S	3			BBB	27	2	7
6	SHEFFIELD UNIVERSITY	◆◆	10	47	ECONOMICS 8/(13 D.HONS OPT) 26	J	3/4						
6	YORK UNIVERSITY	◆◆	26	67	ECONOMICS	S	3			BBC	541	64	12
6	YORK UNIVERSITY	◆◆	26	67	ECONOMICS & FINANCE	S	3			BBC	266	7	3
6	YORK UNIVERSITY	◆◆	26	67	ECONOMICS/ECONOMETRICS (EQUAL)	S	3	+		BBB			
6	YORK UNIVERSITY	◆◆	26	67	ECONOMICS/ECONOMIC STATISTICS	S	3	+		BBB	28	3	11
6	YORK UNIVERSITY	◆◆	26	67	ECONOMICS/EDUCATION	S	3			BBC	9		
6	YORK UNIVERSITY	◆◆	26	67	ECONOMICS/PHILOSOPHY (EQUAL)	S	3			BBB			
6	YORK UNIVERSITY	◆◆	26	67	ECONOMICS/POLITICS (EQUAL)	S	3			BBB			
6	YORK UNIVERSITY	◆◆	26	67	ECONOMICS/SOCIOLOGY (EQUAL)	S	3			BBC-BCC			
6	YORK UNIVERSITY	◆◆	26	67	ECON/ECON & SOC HIST (EQUAL)	S	3			BBC			
6	YORK UNIVERSITY	◆◆	26	67	HISTORY/ECONOMICS	S	3			BBC	67	4	6
6	YORK UNIVERSITY	◆◆	26	67	MATHEMATICS/ECONOMICS	S	3	+		BBC	74	15	20
7	CENTRAL LANCS UNIVERSITY	◆◆	41	92	ECONOMICS	S	3			16	549	29	
7	LANCASTER UNIVERSITY	◆◆	62	62	ACCOUNTING-ECONOMICS	S	3			22			
7	LANCASTER UNIVERSITY	◆◆	62	62	ECONOMICS	S	3	‡		22	329	47	14
7	LANCASTER UNIVERSITY	◆◆	62	62	ECONOMICS WITH JAPANESE STUDIES	S	4	‡		20			
7	LANCASTER UNIVERSITY	◆◆	62	62	ECONOMICS (& 14 OPT) 24	S	3			20-22			
7	LANCASTER UNIVERSITY	◆◆	62	62	MANAGEMENT SCIENCE (ECON)	S	3			22	329	47	14
7	L'POOL JOHN MOORES UNIVERSITY	☐◆	69	30	ECONOMICS & BUSINESS	J	3			16-18			
7	L'POOL JOHN MOORES UNIVERSITY	☐◆	69	30	ECONOMICS & FINANCIAL MANAGEMENT	J	3			12	NEW		

	University				Course							
7	L'POOL JOHN MOORES UNIVERSITY	□◆	69	30	HISTORY & ECONOMICS	J	3		12			
7	L'POOL JOHN MOORES UNIVERSITY	□◆	69	30	HUMAN GEOGRAPHY & ECONOMICS	J	3		14-16			
7	L'POOL JOHN MOORES UNIVERSITY	□◆	69	30	INTERNATIONAL MANAGEMENT & ECONOMICS	J	3		16-18	NEW		
7	L'POOL JOHN MOORES UNIVERSITY	□◆	69	30	MARKETING & ECONOMICS	J	3		16			
7	L'POOL JOHN MOORES UNIVERSITY	□◆	69	30	POLITICS & ECONOMICS	J	3		12			
7	LIVERPOOL UNIVERSITY	●◆	22	78	BUSINESS ECONOMICS	S	3	+£	BCC			
7	LIVERPOOL UNIVERSITY	●◆	22	78	BUSINESS ECONOMICS & COMPUTER SCIENCE	J	3	+£	CCC			
7	LIVERPOOL UNIVERSITY	●◆	22	78	ECONOMETRICS & MATHEMATICAL ECONOMICS	J	3	+	BCC	27	8	30
7	LIVERPOOL UNIVERSITY	●◆	22	78	ECONOMICS	S	3	+£	BCC	317	25	8
7	LIVERPOOL UNIVERSITY	●◆	22	78	ECONOMICS & COMPUTER SCIENCE	J	3	+£	CCC			
7	LIVERPOOL UNIVERSITY	●◆	22	78	ECONOMICS & ECONOMIC HISTORY	J	3	‡	BCC			
7	LIVERPOOL UNIVERSITY	●◆	22	78	ECONOMICS & MATHEMATICS	J	3	+	BCC			
7	LIVERPOOL UNIVERSITY	●◆	22	78	ECONOMICS & MATHS STATS	J	3	+	BCC			
7	LIVERPOOL UNIVERSITY	●◆	22	78	FINANCIAL ECONOMICS	S	3	+£	BCC	99	7	7
7	LIVERPOOL UNIVERSITY	●◆	22	78	MANAGEMENT ECONOMICS & ACCOUNTING	J	3	+£	BCC			
7	MANCHESTER METRO UNIVERSITY	□◆	91	3	ECON-MAITRISE ECONOMETRICS	S	4	‡	CCD	NEW		
7	MANCHESTER METRO UNIVERSITY	□◆	91	3	ECONOMICS (BA HONS)	S	3		18-12	1284	95	7
7	MANCHESTER METRO UNIVERSITY	□◆	91	3	ECONOMICS (BSc HONS)	S	3	‡	18-12	NEW		
7	MANCHESTER METRO UNIVERSITY	□◆	91	3	ECONOMICS (& 11 COMB OPT) 28	J	3/4		18-12			
7	MANCHESTER METRO UNIVERSITY	□◆	91	3	ECONOMICS-MAITRISE (DIJON)	S	4	‡	CCD			
7	MANCHESTER METRO UNIVERSITY	□◆	91	3	INTERNATIONAL ECONOMIC STUDIES (CAEN)	S	4	‡	CCD	157	10	6
7	MANCHESTER METRO UNIVERSITY	□◆	91	3	INTERNATIONAL ECONOMIC STUDIES (MURCIA)	S	4	‡	CCD	NEW		
7	MANCHESTER UNIVERSITY	●◆	7	67	AGRICULTURAL ECONOMICS	S	3		BBC	27		
7	MANCHESTER UNIVERSITY	●◆	7	67	ECONOMICS HISTORY & ECONOMICS	S	3	‡	BCC	22	3	14
7	MANCHESTER UNIVERSITY	●◆	7	67	ECONOMICS (2 COURSES)	S	3		BBC	904	17	2
7	SALFORD UNIVERSITY	●◆	88	19	BIOCHEMISTRY & ECONOMICS	J	3	4 ‡	CCD-BCC			
7	SALFORD UNIVERSITY	●◆	88	19	BUSINESS ECONOMICS	S	3		BCC	244	27	11
7	SALFORD UNIVERSITY	●◆	88	19	CHEMISTRY & ECONOMICS	J	3	4 ‡	CCD-BCC			

TABLE C – ECONOMICS COURSES (Continued)

REGION	NAME	TYPE	VALUE ADDED	EMPLOYMENT	SUBJECT	TYPE	DURATION	SANDWICH	SUBJECTS REQ	GRADES REQ	APPLY		% GET ON
7	SALFORD UNIVERSITY	●●	88	19	COMPUTER SCIENCE & ECONOMICS	J	3	4	‡	CCD-BCC			
7	SALFORD UNIVERSITY	●●	88	19	ECONOMICS	S	3			BCC	155	23	15
7	SALFORD UNIVERSITY	●●	88	19	ECONOMICS & MATHS	J	3	4	‡	CCD-BCC			
7	SUNDERLAND UNIVERSITY	●●	75	94	ECONOMICS	S	3		12		167	67	40
7	SUNDERLAND UNIVERSITY	●●	75	94	ECONOMICS (& 13 COMB OPT) 27	S	3/4						
8	QUEEN'S UNIVERSITY BELFAST	●●	18	55	AGRICULTURAL ECONOMICS & MGT	S	3			CCC	124	20	16
8	QUEEN'S UNIVERSITY BELFAST	●●	18	55	BSc ECONOMICS	S	3			BCC	389	54	14
8	ULSTER UNIVERSITY	●◆	69	30	APPLIED ECONOMICS	S	3	4		BCC	394	22	6
8	ULSTER UNIVERSITY	●◆	69	30	GOVERNMENT & ECONOMICS	S	3			BCC	NEW		
8	ULSTER UNIVERSITY	●◆	69	30	LAW & ECONOMICS	S	3			BBC	NEW		
9	CARDIFF UNIVERSITY	●◆	19	74	ACCOUNTING & ECONOMICS	S	3			BBC			
9	CARDIFF UNIVERSITY	●●	19	74	BUS ECONOMICS WITH FR,GER,IT,SPAN	S	4			BBC	NEW		
9	CARDIFF UNIVERSITY	●●	19	74	BUSINESS ECONOMICS	S	3			BBC	179	23	13
9	CARDIFF UNIVERSITY	●●	19	74	ECONOMICS	S	3			BBC	145	25	17
9	CARDIFF UNIVERSITY	●●	19	74	ECONOMICS WITH FRENCH, GER, ITAL, SPAN	S	4			BBC	NEW		
9	CARDIFF UNIVERSITY	●●	19	74	ECONOMICS & MANAGEMENT STUDIES	S	3			BBC			
9	CARDIFF UNIVERSITY	●●	19	74	ECONOMICS & (14 OPT J. HONS) 39	J	3			BBC			
9	SWANSEA UNIVERSITY	●●	63	86	ECONOMICS & (17 JOINT OPT) 40	J	3		8				
9	SWANSEA UNIVERSITY	●●	63	86	ECONOMICS (BA)	S	3			BCC-BCC	141	28	20
9	SWANSEA UNIVERSITY	●●	63	86	ECONOMICS (BSc HONS)	S	3			BBC-BCC	22	3	14
9	SWANSEA UNIVERSITY	●●	63	86	ECONOMICS (SGL HONS)	S	3			BCC-BCC	105	19	18

9	UNIV COLL OF N.WALES, BANGOR	♦♦	15	88	ECONOMICS	S	3		BCC	227	18	8
9	UNIV COLL OF N.WALES, BANGOR	♦♦	15	88	ECONOMICS/FR(SYLL A)	J	4		BCC			
9	UNIV COLL OF N.WALES, BANGOR	♦	15	88	ECONOMICS/FR(SYLL B)	J	4		BCC			
9	UNIV COLL OF N.WALES, BANGOR	♦♦	15	88	ECONOMICS/GERMAN RUSSIAN	J	4		BCC			
9	UNIV COLL OF N.WALES, BANGOR	♦♦	15	88	ECONOMICS/HISTORY	J	3		BCC			
9	UNIV COLL OF N.WALES, BANGOR	♦♦	15	88	ECONOMICS/MATHS	J	3		18			
9	UNIV COLL OF N.WALES, BANGOR	♦	15	88	ECONOMICS/MODERN LANGUAGES	J	4		18			
9	UNIV COLL OF N.WALES, BANGOR	♦♦	15	88	ECONOMICS/SOC POL	J	3		BCC			
9	UNIV COLL OF N.WALES, BANGOR	♦	15	88	ECONOMICS/SOCIOLOGY	J	3		BCC			
9	UNIV OF WALES, ABERYSTWYTH	♦♦	35	86	ACCOUNTING & FINANCE & ECONOMICS	J	3		BCC			
9	UNIV OF WALES, ABERYSTWYTH	♦♦	35	86	AGRICULTURAL ECONOMICS	S	3	‡	BCC	45	3	7
9	UNIV OF WALES, ABERYSTWYTH	♦♦	35	86	COMPUTER SCIENCE/ECONOMICS	J	3	‡	20			
9	UNIV OF WALES, ABERYSTWYTH	♦♦	35	86	ECONOMICS	S	3	‡	BCC	221	40	18
9	UNIV OF WALES, ABERYSTWYTH	♦♦	35	86	ECONOMICS & ECON & SOC HIST	S	3		BCC			
9	UNIV OF WALES, ABERYSTWYTH	♦♦	35	86	ECONOMICS & INTERNATIONAL POLITICS	S	3		BCC			
9	UNIV OF WALES, ABERYSTWYTH	♦♦	35	86	ECONOMICS & LAW	S	3		BBB/BBC			
9	UNIV OF WALES, ABERYSTWYTH	♦♦	35	86	ECONOMICS & MARKETING	S	3		BCC			
9	UNIV OF WALES, ABERYSTWYTH	♦♦	35	86	ECONOMICS & POLITICS	S	3		BCC			
9	UNIV OF WALES, ABERYSTWYTH	♦♦	35	86	ECONOMICS & STATISTICS	S	3		BCC	8		
9	UNIV OF WALES, ABERYSTWYTH	♦♦	35	88	ECONOMICS (BSc)	S	3		BCC	11	1	
9	UNIV OF WALES, ABERYSTWYTH	♦♦	35	86	ECONOMICS/AGRICULTURAL ECONOMICS	J	3		BCC	16	2	
9	UNIV OF WALES, ABERYSTWYTH	♦♦	35	86	ECONOMICS/FRENCH, GER, ITAL, SPAN	J	4		BCC			
9	UNIV OF WALES, ABERYSTWYTH	♦♦	35	86	ECONOMICS/GEOGRAPHY	J	3		BCC			
9	UNIV OF WALES, ABERYSTWYTH	♦♦	35	86	ECONOMICS/HISTORY	J	3		BCC			
9	UNIV OF WALES, ABERYSTWYTH	♦♦	35	86	ECONOMICS/INFO & LIB ST	J	3		BCC			
9	UNIV OF WALES, ABERYSTWYTH	♦♦	35	86	ECONOMICS/MATHS	J	3		CCC			
9	UNIV OF WALES, ABERYSTWYTH	♦♦	35	86	ECONOMICS/WELSH HISTORY	J	3		BCC			
10	ABERDEEN UNIVERSITY	♦♦	47	41	ACCOUNTING-ECONOMICS	J	4	‡	BBC	5070	757	15

TABLE C - ECONOMICS COURSES (Continued)

REGION	NAME	VA TYPE	VALUE ADDED	EMPLOYMENT	SUBJECT	TYPE	DURATION	SANDWICH	SUBJECTS REQ	GRADES REQ	APPLY	GET ON	%
10	ABERDEEN UNIVERSITY	◆◆	47	41	AGRICULTURAL ECONOMICS	S	4	‡		CDD	175	46	26
10	ABERDEEN UNIVERSITY	◆◆	47	41	AGRICULTURAL ECON-MANAGEMENT STUDIES	J	4	‡		BBC	5070	757	15
10	ABERDEEN UNIVERSITY	◆◆	47	41	ECONOMIC SCIENCE	S	4	‡		BBC	5070	757	15
10	ABERDEEN UNIVERSITY	◆◆	47	41	ECONOMICS (& 10 COMB OPT) 30	J	4	‡		BBC	5070	757	15
10	ABERDEEN UNIVERSITY	◆◆	47	41	LLB (WITH OPTION IN ECONOMICS)	J	3/4	‡		BBB	951	157	17
10	DUNDEE INSTITUTE	✷◆	N/A	N/A	APPLIED ECONOMICS	S	3/4	‡		DD			27
10	DUNDEE UNIVERSITY	◆◆	9	30	CHEMISTRY & ECONOMICS	S	4	‡		BC-CDD	2516	223	9
10	DUNDEE UNIVERSITY	◆◆	9	30	COMPUTER SCIENCE & ECONOMICS	S	4	‡		BC-CDD	2516	223	9
10	DUNDEE UNIVERSITY	◆◆	9	30	CONTEMP EUR ST-ECONOMICS	J	4			BCC	3407	373	11
10	DUNDEE UNIVERSITY	◆◆	9	30	CONTEMP EUR ST-FINANCIAL ECONOMICS	J	4			BCC	3407	373	11
10	DUNDEE UNIVERSITY	◆◆	9	30	ECONOMICS	S	4			BCC	3407	373	11
10	DUNDEE UNIVERSITY	◆◆	9	30	ECONOMICS & (10 OPT J. HONS) 29	J	4			BCC	NEW		
10	DUNDEE UNIVERSITY	◆◆	9	30	FINANCIAL ECONOMICS	S	4			BCC	3407	373	11
10	DUNDEE UNIVERSITY	◆◆	9	30	FINANCIAL ECONOMICS & (7 OPT J.HONS) 29	J	4			BCC	NEW		
10	DUNDEE UNIVERSITY	◆◆	9	30	MATHS & ECONOMICS	S	4	+		BCC	2516	223	9
10	DUNDEE UNIVERSITY	◆◆	9	30	STATISTICS & ECONOMICS	S	4	+		BCC	2516	223	9
10	EDINBURGH UNIVERSITY	◆◆	26	50	AGRICULTURAL ECONOMICS	S	4	‡		CDD			
10	EDINBURGH UNIVERSITY	◆◆	26	50	ARABIC & ECONOMICS	J	4	‡		BBC			
10	EDINBURGH UNIVERSITY	◆◆	26	50	BUSINESS STUDIES & ECONOMICS	J	4			BBC			
10	EDINBURGH UNIVERSITY	◆◆	26	50	ECONOMICS	S	4			BBC	206	25	12
10	EDINBURGH UNIVERSITY	◆◆	26	50	ECONOMICS & (11 OPT MA HONS 31	S	4			BBC			

	Institution				Course				Grade			
10	GLASGOW UNIVERSITY	●◆	69	67	AGRICULTURAL ECONOMICS	S	4		BCC	5729	945	16
10	HERIOT-WATT UNIVERSITY	●◆	22	50	ECONOMICS	S	4		CCC			
10	HERIOT-WATT UNIVERSITY	●◆	22	50	ECONOMICS & FRENCH/GERMAN	J	3/4	L	BBC			
10	HERIOT-WATT UNIVERSITY	●◆	22	50	ECONOMICS & FRENCH/RUSSIAN	J	3/4	L	BBC			
10	HERIOT-WATT UNIVERSITY	●◆	22	50	ECONOMICS & FRENCH/SPANISH	J	3/4	L	BBC			
10	HERIOT-WATT UNIVERSITY	●◆	22	50	ECONOMICS & RUSSIAN/GERMAN	J	3/4	L	BBC			
10	HERIOT-WATT UNIVERSITY	●◆	22	50	ECONOMICS & SPANISH/GERMAN	J	3/4	L	BBC			
10	HERIOT-WATT UNIVERSITY	●◆	22	50	ECONOMICS & SPANISH/RUSSIAN	J	3/4	L	BBC			
10	HERIOT-WATT UNIVERSITY	●◆	22	50	MATHS WITH ECONOMICS	S	4		CCE	56	10	18
10	STIRLING UNIVERSITY	●●	31	41	ECONOMICS	S	4		BC-CCC	260	28	11
10	STIRLING UNIVERSITY	●●	31	41	ECONOMICS (& 20 COMB OPT) 33	S	4		BC-CCC			
10	STIRLING UNIVERSITY	●◆	31	41	MATHS & ITS APPLICATIONS WITH ECONOMICS	S	4	‡	BC-CCC	7	2	29
10	STRATHCLYDE UNIVERSITY	●◆	88	41	MATHEMATICS WITH ECONOMICS	S	3 4		CDD	38	8	21
10	ST.ANDREWS UNIVERSITY	*◆	7	26	ECONOMICS	S	4		BBB	4588	462	10
10	ST.ANDREWS UNIVERSITY	*◆	7	26	ECONOMICS & MANAGEMENT SCIENCE	S	4	+	BBC	3073	431	14
10	ST.ANDREWS UNIVERSITY	*◆	7	26	ECONOMICS (SC)	S	4		BBC	3073	431	14
10	ST.ANDREWS UNIVERSITY	*◆	7	26	ECONOMICS (& 21 OPT) 32	S	3/4		BBC	4588	462	10
10	ST.ANDREWS UNIVERSITY	*◆	7	26	ECONOMICS (& 5 LANG OPT) 32	S	5		BBB	NEW		
10	ST.ANDREWS UNIVERSITY	*◆	7	26	MATHS & ECONOMICS (SC)	S	3	+	BCC	3073	431	14
10	ST.ANDREWS UNIVERSITY	*◆	7	26	PSYCHOLOGY & ECONOMICS	S	4		BBC	3073	431	14

SUPPLEMENTARY INFORMATION TO THE TABLES

This section shows the options that can be studied with the main subject you have chosen. For an explanation see page 28.

ACCOUNTANCY

1 BOLTON INST
Acc & Maths (10-12); Acc & Art & Des, Biol, Bus St, Comm St, Comput, Envir St, Eur Cult St & Soc St, Eur Lang, Gend & Wom St, Hist, Leis St, Peace & War St, Phil, Theatre St, Tour St, Urb & Cult St, Vis Arts (12); Lit (12-14); Psy (14)

2 ABERDEEN
Acc-Fr, Ger, Hisp St, (4/5 yrs); Acc-Geog, Mgt St, Phil, Soc Res, Soc, Stats (4 yrs)

3 OXFORD BROOKES
Acc & Fin/BA & Mgt, Cater Mgt, Engl St, Fine Art, Hlth & Exec St, Hist, Ret Mgt (3 yrs); Fr Lan & Cntl St, Fr Lang & Lit, Ger Lang & Cntl St, Ger Lang & Lit (4 yrs);Anthrop & Acc & Fin, Appl Stats, Biol, Cartog, Chem, Comput Maths, Comput, Econ, Educ St, Envir Sc, Envir Biol, Food Sc & Nut, Geog, Geol, Geo Tech, Hist of Art, Intell Sys, Law, Mkting Mgt, Maths, Microelect Sys, Music, Phy Sc, Phy, Plan St, Polit, Psy, Publ, Soc, Tour, Vis St (3 yrs)

4 ABERYSTWYTH
Acc/Appl Maths, Maths, Pure Maths, Stats (BCC); Comput Sc, Phy, Phy wth Elect (I)

BUSINESS STUDIES

5 ROEHAMPTON
BS/Appl Comput & Info Sys, Consum Sc & Tech, Dance St, Drama & Theat St, Educ St, Engl Lang, Engl Envir St, Geog, Heal St, Hist, Maths wth Stats, Maths, Music, Prod Mgt St, Psy, Soc Admin, Soc Biol, Soc, Sports St, Wom St, Theol & Rel St (3 yrs); Fr (4 yrs)

6 W.LONDON INST
Amer St & BS, BS & Drama, Earth Sc, Engl, Geog, Geol, Hist, Music, Rel St, Sports St

7 BEDFORD COLL
Bus St wth Art & Des, Eur St, Eur St wth Fr, Eur St wth Ger, Geog, Maths, Soc, (12, New); Dance & Drama, Envir St, Hist, Hist/Soc, Lang & Lit, Leis & Rec St, Sports St/Sc (12); Hist wth Bus St (12, New); Eur St (3FT,4SW); Dance & Drama, Envir St, Hist/Soc, Lang & Lit, (12); Leis & Rec St, Sports St/Sc (14); Eur St wth BS (12, 3-4 yrs)

8 KEELE UNIV
Anc Hist & BA, Appl Soc St, (New, BBC); Astrop & BA (New, BCC), BA & Biochem, Fr, Ger, Med & Biol Chem, Russ, Soc, (BCC); Russ St & BA, Geog (BCC)BA & Law (BBB); Polit & BA, HR Mgt (BBC); BA & EnvirMgt, Soc (BCC)

9 BOLTON INST.
Bus St & Maths, Eur Lang (10-12), Acc & Bus St, Biol, Phil, Tour St, Art & Des Hist, Comput, Eur Cult & Soc St, Gen & Wom St, Hist, Leis St, Lit (12); Psy (14); Comm St & Bus St, Envir St, Peace & War St, Theatre, Urb & Cult St, Vis Arts (12)

10 STAFFORDSHIRE
BS & Geog, Intl Pol & Admin, Intl Rel, Leg St, Pol St, Polit, Soc (BC-BCC); Fr,
Ger, Span, (3 FT, 4 SW, BC-BCC); Info Sys (BC-BCC); Phy, Chem, (CC-DD); Elect
(DD)

11 SUNDERLAND
Geog/Bus, Geol, Med St, Psy, Soc (New), Polit/Bus

12 STIRLING
BS & Flm & Med St, (ABB); BS/Polit, Psy, Soc Pol, Soc, Educ, Econ (BBC); BS/Fin
St, Fr, Ger, Jap, Span Lang, (BCC); Maths, Comput St, (BC-CCC); Span, Ger,
Fr/BS (BCC)

13 ANGLIA PO/U
Bus/Soc Pol, (3yrs,12,New); Comm St (3yrs,14); Chem, Maths, RT Comput Sys (3
yrs,8); Instrum Elect (3yrs,8,New); Geol (10,New); Eur Thou & Lit (12); Contem
Eur St, Geog, Graph Art, Hist, Art Hist, Music, Polit, Soc, Wom St, (3yrs,14), Fr,
Ger, Ital, Span (4yrs,14) Law (16)

14 CANT CHRISTCH
Bus St & Engl, Rad, Flm & TV, (BB); Bus St & Am St, Hist, Music, Relig St, Soc &
Educ St, Art, Tour (New, CC); Sports Sc, Geog (CC); IT, Maths, Sc, Engl & Bus St,
Rad, Flm & TV, (BB); Bus St & Am St, Hist, Music, Relig St, Soc & Educ St, Art,
Tour (New, CC); Sports Sc, Geog (CC); IT, Maths, Sc,

15 SUFFOLK COLL
BS wth Acc, Bus Law, Info Tech, Mgt, Mkting, Pers,Bus & Fin (Acc), Eur Bus, Fin
Ser, Intl Ship & Tde, Mkting, Pers, Tour

16 UNIV E.LONDON
BS/ Art Des & Flm Hist, Biochem & Biotech, Cult St, Indep St (Soc Sc), Micro &
Parasit, Polit St, Biol Sc (New), Soc Anthrop, Soc SciDes/BS, Econ, Educ & Comm
St, Envir St, Eur St, Fine Art, Heal St, Hist, Info Tech, Law, Ling, Liter, Maths Sc
& Comput, Med, Phsio & Pharm, Pop Cult, Psy, Psychsoc St, Soc Pol Res, Soc,
Third World St, Urb St, Wom St (3 yrs); Fr, Ger, Ital, Span, (3-4 yrs)

17 CHELT & GLOUC
Bus Comput Sys &/wth Bus St, Bus Info Tech &/wth Bus St, (3 yrs, 8-12); wth
Maths (4 yrs, 8-12); Bus St & Cater Mgt 4 yrs, 10); Bus St & Fin Mgt, Hotel Mgt,
Leis Mgt, Tour Mgt, wth Bus Comput Sys, Bus Info Tech, Cater Mgt, Ear Res,
Envir Pol, Fin Serv, Hotel Mgt, Leis Mgt, Lang (FR), Recr St, Tour Mgt (4 yrs, 12)

18 OXFORD BROOKES
Acc & Fin/BA & Mgt, Anthrop, App Stats, Biol, Chem, Comput Maths, Econ, Educ,
Envir Biol, Food Sc & Nut, Geog, Geol, Geotech, Hist of Art, Hist, Intell Sys, Law,
Mkting Mgt, Maths, Micro Sys, Music, Phar St, Polit, Psy, Pub, Soc, Tour, Vis St;
BA & Mgt/Cartog, Cater Mgt, Eng St, Fine Art, Fr/Ger Lang & Lit, Fr/Ger Lang &
Cntl St, Heal & Exer Sc, Phy Sc, Phy; BA & Ret Mgt; BA/Envir Sc

19 PLYMOUTH
Biol (Appl Plant Sc) wth BS, Biotech, Cell Biol & Immun, Envir, Human,
Microbiol

ECONOMICS

20 LON-QM&WC
Law & Econ (3 yrs, BBC); Hisp St, Russ (3/4 yrs, BCC); Fr, Ger (4, BCC); Phy (3 yrs, CCC); Econ & Hist (BCD); Econ & Polit, Stats & Maths (BCC)

21 LON-ROYAL HOL
Mgt St wth Econ (BBB); Maths, Music, Maths wth Econ & Mgt (3 yrs, BBC-BCC); Fr, Ger, Ital (4 yrs, BCC); Greek, Latin, Soc Pol, Soc, Class St, Anc Hist (3yrs, BCC); Econ wth Class St, Soc Pol (BCC, New); Fr, Ger, Gk, Ital, Latin, Span, Mgt St, Maths, Music, Polit, Pub Admin, Soc (3 yrs, BCC); Jap (4 yrs, BCC)

22 UNIV E. LONDON
Bus Info Sys/ Econ, Design, Educ & Comm St, Envir St,Eur St, Fine Art, Health St, Hist, Info Tech, Law, Ling, Lit, Math ,Stats & Comput, Med St, Physio & Pharm, Pop Cult, Psy, Psycosoc St, Soc Pol Res, Pub Sect Econ, Soc, Third Wor St, Urb St, Wom St (3 yrs); Fr, Ger, Ital (3/4 yrs); Econ/Art Des & Film Hist, Bioch & Biotech, Biol Sc, Bus St, Cult St, Indep St (Soc Sc), Micro & Parasit, Polit St, Soc. Anthrop, Soc Scs,

23 KEELE UNIV
Class St & Econ, Engl (BBC); Am St & Econ, Comput Sc, Geol, HR Mgt, Intl Hist, Music, Russ St, (BCC); Anc Hist, Astroph (New, BCC); Phy (BDC); Econ & Phil, Polit, (BBC); Class St, (3 yrs, BCC); Elect Music, FR, Ger, Geog,Latin, Maths, Russ, Stats (3/4 yrs, BCC); Biochem, Chem, Med & Biochem (3/4 yrs, BCD)Crimin & Econ, Psy, Law (3/4 yrs, BBB); Soc (BBC); Intl Polit, (BCC); Appl Soc St (New, BCC)Fr/Ger & Econ, Fr/Russ or Russ St, Ger/Russ or Russ St (3/4 yrs, BBB)

24 LANCASTER
Econ & Mod Hist (20); Econ – Maths, Phil (20-22)); Geog, IT, Mkting, Oper Res, Polit, Soc (22); Fr, Ger, Ital, Span, Acc (4 yrs, 22)

25 LEEDS UNIV
Econ-Mgt St, Polit, (3 yrs, BBB); Polit wth Am St, (4 yrs, BBB); Geog, Hist, Hist wth Am St,, Phil, (3yrs, BBC); Fr, Ger, Russ, (4 yrs, BBC); Maths, Stats (3/4 yrs, BBC); Econ & Soc Hist (3 yrs, BCC); Soc (3 yrs, 22); Soc Pol (3 yrs, 20)

26 UNIV SHEFFIELD
Econ & Geog, Jap St, Phil, Polit, Soc Pol, Soc (3 yrs, BBB); Korean St (4 yrs, BBB); Maths, Stats (3 yrs, BBC); Fr/Econ, Ger, Russ, Span (4 yrs, BBC)

27 SUNDERLAND
Fr/Econ, Ger (4 yrs, 6-8); Maths, Comput, (3 yrs, 6-8); Chem & Econ, Geol, Geog, Hist, Phil, Physiol (3 yrs, 8-10); Polit, Psy, Soc (10)

28 MAN METROP U.
Econ/Appl Maths, Chem. Comput Sc, Lang; Envir St/Econ, Eur St, Geog, Manuf, Mats Sc, Print & Photo Tech, Psy (3 yrs)

29 UNIV DUNDEE
Econ/Educ, Mgt, Fin Econ, (New); Envir St, Geog, Mod Hist, Polit Sc, Psy, Soc Pol ; MathsEnvir Sc/Fin Econ; Fin Econ/Geog, Mod Hist, Polit Sc, Psy, Soc Pol; Mgt (New)

30 ABERDEEN
Econ/Ag Econ, Econ Hist, IR, Mgt St, Maths, Phil, Polit,Stats (4 yrs); Econ/Fr,Ger (4/5 yrs)

31 EDINBURGH
Econ & Acc, Econ Hist, Soc,(BBC); Stats, Maths (BBC); Law, Polit (BBB); Geog & Econ, Phil, Soc Pol (BBC); Law (ABB)

32 ST ANDREWS
Econ/Intl Rel, (4 yrs, ABB); Geog, Hist (Anc, Econ & Soc, Med, Mod), Logic & Met, Mgt St, Maths (Arts), Mod Lang, Fr, Ger, Span, Arab, Russ, Moral Phil, Phil, Psy, Soc Anthrop, Stats (Arts), (4 yrs, BBB); Stats (Sc) (3/4, BCC); Bib St/ Econ (4 yrs, BBB) Mod Lang, Fr, Ger, Span, Arab, Russ wth yr abroad (4 yrs, BBB)

33 STIRLING
Econ/Film & Med St (ABB); Fin St, Hist, Mgt Sc, Polit St (BCC); Bus Law, Educ, Envir Sc, Fr Lang, Ger or Ger Lang, Jap Lang, Maths, Phil, Soc, Span Lang (BC-CCC); Econ/Mkting (BC-CC); Acc/Econ, Bus St (BBC); Comput Sc, HR Mgt (BC-CCC)

34 ANGLIA/POLY
Bus Econ/Eur Thou & Lit (12,New), Engl (16) Maths/Bus Econ (8), Music, Soc Pol (12,New) Contemp Eur St, Geog, Graphic Arts(New), Hist, Polit, Soc, Womens's St(14), Law (16)

35 KENT
Econ/Law (26); Polit & Govt, Soc Anthrop, Soc Pol & Admin, Soc (BCC)

36 READING
Acc & Econ, (3 yrs, BBC); Fr (4 yrs, BBC); Hist, Intl Rel, Maths, Polit (3 yrs, BCC); Iral, Ger, (4 yrs, CCC); Chem wth Econ (3 yrs, CCC), Chem wth Econ(yr in Eur) (4 yrs, CC); Econ & Economet, Soc (3 yrs , BCC)

37 OXFORD BROOKES
Comput Maths/Econ, Educ St, Envir Biol, Envir Sc, Food Sc, & Nut, Geog, Geol, Geotech, Hist of Art, Hist, Intell Sys, Law, Mkting Mgt, Maths, Microelect Sys, Music, Phy Sc, Phy, Polit, Psy, Pub, Ret Mgt, Soc, Tour, Vis St (3 yrs); Econ/Acc & Fin, Anthrop, Appl Stats, Biol, BA & Mgt, Cartog, Cater Mgt, Comput, Engl St, Fine Art (3 yrs); Fr, Fr Lang & Contemp St, Ger/Ger Lang & Contemp St, Ger Lang & Lit, Heal & Exec Sc (4 yrs)

38 PLYMOUTH
Econ (Appl) wth Acc, Geog, Lang, Law, Pol, Psy, Res Manuf & Envir, Soc Pol, Soc Stats, Transp; Geog wth Econ (Appl), Law, Poilt, Psy, Soc Pol, Soc

39 UNIV WALES CARDIFF
Econ/Educ, Hist, Hist of Ideas, Phil, Soc Phil & ApplEth,Welsh, Welsh Hist, Polit, Soc (3 yrs); Fr, Ger, Ital, Port, Span (4 yrs)

40 SWANSEA
Econ & Russ St, /Russ St (3 yrs, 20); /Span (4 yrs, 18-20); /Fr (4 yrs, 20); Econ & Geog (2 courses) (3 yrs, 20-24); /Geog (3 yrs, 20-22); Maths, Polit, Psy, Soc Pol, Soc Stats, Stats, Hist (BCC); Welsh & Econ, Econ Hist, Dev St (BCC)

Other essential books from Trotman's...

The Complete Degree Course Offers 1995
by Brian Heap
25th Edition
This essential book for applicants to higher education includes points requirements for entry to all first degree courses, advice on how to choose a course and institution, information on how to complete the new section 10 on the UCAS form and much more.
Price: £14.95
Published April 1994

How To Choose Your Degree Course
by Brian Heap
4th Edition
The long awaited new edition of this book contains general advice on how to go about choosing which degree subject to study, looking at A-level subjects and their related courses, and at career groups and specific careers.
Price: £11.95
Published April 1994

How To Choose Your Higher National Diploma Course
Second Edition
This extensively revised and updated publication provides information on: entrance requirements, course descriptions, selection criteria and procedures, intake numbers and applications received, sponsorship and work placements, employment statistics as well as information on GNVQs and NVQs.
Price: £14.95

Order Form (please photocopy)

Please send me the following books:

		Qty	Total
Degree Course Offers 1995	£14.95 + 2.20 p+p	_____	£_____
How To Choose Your Degree Course	£11.95 + 2.20 p+p	_____	£_____
How To Choose Your HND Course	£14.95 + 2.20 p+p	_____	£_____
		Total	**£_____**

Please call us on 081-332-2132 for Access and Visa orders and postage and packing rates for multiple copy orders.

Trotman books are available through good bookshops everywhere.

Cash Orders: Please make your cheque payable to **Trotman & Company** and send it to: **12 Hill Rise, Richmond, Surrey, TW10 6UA.**
Credit Orders: only for schools'/organisations' orders of **over £35.** Please attatch your **official order form** to ours. The original invoice will be sent with the books, payment is due within 28 days.